River Trilogy

Travels Down Three
of the
World's
Great Rivers

Jono Lineen

Pottersfield Press, Lawrencetown Beach, Nova Scotia, Canada

National Library of Canada Cataloguing in Publication Data

Lineen, Jono

      River trilogy: travels down three of the world's great rivers

      ISBN 1-895900-45-X

1. Ganges River (India and Bangladesh) – Description and travel.
2. Rhine River – Description and travel.
3. Tatshenshini River – Description and travel.
4. Lineen, Jono – Journeys.
I. Title.
G465.L554 2001   910.4   C2001-902012-0

Pottersfield Press gratefully acknowledges the ongoing support of the Nova Scotia Department of Tourism and Culture, Cultural Affairs Division, as well as The Canada Council for the Arts. We acknowledge the financial support of the Government of Canada through the Book Publishing Industry Development Program for our publishing activities.

Cover photograph by Jono Lineen
Cover design: Jono Lineen and Gail LeBlanc, Dal Graphics

Pottersfield Press
83 Leslie Road
East Lawrencetown
Nova Scotia, Canada, B2Z 1P6
To order, telephone: 1-800-NIMBUS9 (1-800-646-2879) toll free
Website: www.pottersfieldpress.com

THE CANADA COUNCIL FOR THE ARTS SINCE 1957 | LE CONSEIL DES ARTS DU CANADA DEPUIS 1957

Tourism and Culture

Contents

Any book is the product of more than one mind and this is especially true of a work such as this, one that crosses so many physical, cultural and psychological borders. It would have been impossible without the help of a large group of friends and family. Thanks to Mum, Peter, Katrina, Dad, and Gareth. To the family Schertler, especially Rochus and also Leo on the Rhine. To Adam on the Tat. To Kaja, Sunderlal Bahaguna, Swami Sachiananda, and Rana Singh on the Ganges. To Fin Donnelly for trail blazing, to Mike C. for encouragement, to Fin F. for editing, to Lesley Choyce for faith, and to Stuart L. for inspiration.

Introduction

I remember once flying from Bangkok to Calcutta. It was August and the monsoon season had given the sky a heavy sullen look. The plane had been floating through a nether world of gray cloud for most of the flight and visibility was limited to the dim green and red lights flashing on the wing tips. But as we moved over western Bangladesh, the cumulous cover had miraculously parted and below us, sparkling in the late summer sun, lay the delta of the Ganges.

The river had shocked me. It was in full flood and had infiltrated the landscape as far as the eye could see. The channels of the Ganges, the Brahmaputra, the Padma, the Meghna, and the Hooghly had splintered and spread themselves across a nation that had become water. The oblique sun suddenly caught the glistening river world and shot it with a golden glow. The world beneath me took on the bronzed shade of old gold. It was the color of history, mythology, and stories that leave you breathless.

The earth vibrated with the sun's energy and in a sweeping flash the golden light was reflected upwards and into the plane. Inside, the minimal interior was abruptly transformed from a pastel grotto to a shimmering rococo palace. The seats were instantly upholstered in golden silks, the wine in my glass shivered with incandescent light, and the steel watch on my wrist turned to solid gold. My elderly neighbor had turned to me, raised his golden filigreed eyebrows and smiled in recognition of the event, his toothy grin set with glinting rows of perfect golden nuggets.

For that moment, that precious second, the world was the color of dreams.

But almost as suddenly a cloud moved across the sun and I found myself staring down on a monochrome gray landscape so minutely cut with streams that it was difficult to tell where the land ended and the water began.

The delta's intricacy was fathomless and I immediately recalled da Vinci's sketches of the human circulatory system. Like the body's, the Ganges' flow was divided into smaller and smaller arteries, arterioles and capillaries until finally the river and the earth were indistinguishable. It was there, at the point where land and water intersected, that the transmission of the world's energy took place. I was seeing the river as the circulatory system of the world.

Below me, beauty and power had fused in the body of the river. In that single epiphany the Ganga had risen from sea level to 9,200 meters. She had moved from the world of the gods to the inner cosmos of my own psychology. From on high I had seen, like Zeus on Olympus or Shiva on Mount Kailash, the true depth of the river.

Months later on that same trip I found myself at the source of the Ganges. From a rock-strewn moraine field, 4,300 meters up in the Central Himalaya, I watched the Bhagriath Glacier give birth to the river that has nurtured a civilization.

Before me a circle of celestial peaks reached for the heavens. They were the bosom of the Goddess and their smooth icy flanks ran downwards to the hollow that held the advancing glacier. The glacier stopped at my feet and from its frontal face towering blocks of ice, larger than apartment buildings, leaned outwards at precarious angles. It was from the base of those icy fingers, from the point where the water met the earth, that the river emerged.

From a dark frozen grotto a cool joyous flow, bubbling with the effervescence of youth, entered the mortal world. My eyes followed it into the birth canal cave, to the point where it dissolved into blackness, where it receded out of my existence and back into the heart of the mountains.

I could feel it, the sense of birth and giving. The Himalayas, the home of the Hindu gods, had created the Ganges. The pantheon of deities had squeezed it from ice and rock and delivered it to the earth as a gift. The river was an offering, a conduit that insured the well-being of the 300 million people who populate its shores. I dipped my hand into the freezing flow, drank deeply of the gods' moist efforts, and blessed my forehead with a wipe of the chilly residue.

Then I sat in peace and watched the water flow onwards, unfazed by the constant movement but touched by the emotion. I heard a boulder far up the glacier drop from the heights with an artillery crack. The rumble rolled and echoed down the frozen valley and on my cheeks I felt warm tears fall as cold droplets onto my forearm.

At its outlet, at the endpoint of its existence, I had seen the river in all its munificent glory and then at its birth I saw it as the fragile but infinitely potent newborn goddess. The juxtaposition of the two images clicked in me, for I was struck by the similarities between rivers and humans and in the months following that insight a million questions of the waters quietly laid their seed in me. Was the personality that I had seen in the Ganga mirrored and reimaged by the world's millions of other watercourses? Did each of them possess an individuality, a sense of character like that of the Ganges? How did the personality of those rivers affect the people along their banks? How did the earth function in relation to its ever-moving cousin? Why had we humans lost contact with the river, the earthly feature that most defines our everyday lives?

Rivers and spirituality, rivers and industry, rivers and nationalism, rivers of nature, rivers of life, rivers of memory, rivers of time, and rivers of blood. The rivers' many personalities I could see were fluvial renderings of our own thoughts and dreams.

The river had caught me in its flow but the answers that I found to those many queries just led me to more questions, and over the next few years I became absorbed by the water's many forms.

I decided to approach my research in the same way I would get to know a friend. I would sit with them, read with them, walk with them, and talk with them. Eventually I saw that if I wanted to acquaint myself with the river I would have to take longer trips and encounter them in different environments. I realized that if I wanted to understand the water's power I would have to appreciate it on its own terms. I would have to go to the river, not wait for it to come to me.

So I chose three watercourses that I thought best characterized some of the river's many personalities. Then I followed those rivers, slowly and thoughtfully, from their sources to their outlets. I tracked the Ganges from the Himalayas to the Bay of Bengal, I pedaled my bicycle along the Rhine from the Alps to the Atlantic, and I hiked and paddled the Tatshenshini River through the Yukon, British Columbia and Alaska.

In the beginning I had wanted to define and categorize the river hoping in some way that by rationalizing it I could incorporate some of its power within me. But the rivers laughed at those fancies and proved again and again that they are too large to be placed into neatly arranged boxes.

As the years wore on I began to see the river not only as the greatest storyteller but as the most fundamental teacher. For those able to listen every stream has a tale to tell and every river has the wisdom to open another aspect of ourselves. We share the river's fluid dreams and eventually the flow is incorporated into our own bodies. The river is a part of us, it is home.

Ganga/Ganges

Gaumukh in Sanskrit translates as cow's mouth and it is from this, the mouth of Hinduism's most sacred animal, that the river Ganges appears to human eyes.

Gaumukh is the yawning ice cave at the base of the Bhagriath Glacier from which the river emerges. The cavern's shimmering, transluscent frozen walls climb for thirty meters above the water. On its faces are recorded the ice floe's millennia of waxing and waning: the cave is smooth and glossy through some periods, rough and opaque in others. It is a physical reminder of the ages, a calendar of that most precious of commodities — water.

It is fitting that the river should emerge from that gateway. The Central Indian Himalaya is the heartland of Hindu pilgrimage, the geographic altar of the world's billion Hindus. The Ganges is the centerpiece of that mountain icon, and as if to confirm its position it appears miraculously from those ghostly blue confines not as a stream or a brook but as a full-fledged river. To see her there in the first seconds of her earthly existence, pushing the boundaries of what we would rightly think of as a source stream, is to appreciate the Ganga's enigma.

Legends talk of her origins at Mount Kailash in central Tibet, hundreds of kilometers to the northeast. From there she flows underground, gaining size and strength until, in the most dramatic of fashions, she enters the human realm from the bosom of the Bhagriath mountains' cirque of celestial peaks.

Following the rough trail along her banks I watched the water career ahead of me. Tossed along in white abandon, the incessant flow lapped aggressively at the shores pounding the Himalayas' rough stones smooth. The Ganga was in a rush, an appropriate state as the name Ganga stems from the Sanskrit root *gam,* to go. The Ganges is the "swift goer," an idea that the prayers and hymns composed in her honor constantly emphasize. She is the most compassionate of the gods, always first to lend a hand to those in need.

The sheer speed of her early movement is purging. As a rolling stone gathers no moss, no passenger on the nascent Ganga could leave her uncleansed. This ability to purify is the root of the river's connection with her Hindu admirers. To them she is the Mother Goddess, a manifestation of the ultimate purity. For her followers to be with her is to be as close to perfection as is possible in this life.

Down the valley four kilometers from Gaumukh is the first sign of civilization. There at Bhujbasa the Hindu holyman Lal Baba has constructed his ashram, a collection of shrines and dormitories in a widening of a barren, treeless valley at 3,800 meters.

When I arrived the guru and his followers had departed for the winter. My silent greeting party was two saddhus, Hindu renunciates, who were reclining in the courtyard. Heavily swaddled in woolen blankets they were enjoying the bright white winter light. Like a pair of recumbent sunflowers they faced south, leaning to the source of their growth.

When they saw me one of them smiled a crazy, pearl-toothed smile and the other gestured with regal hands for me to take a seat on the stone bench beside him. I gratefully sat down, happy to relieve my tired legs. But this was no time to relax and my host immediately got down to the business of my business: what exactly were my plans in his domain?

His directness was unsettling but he wasn't being intrusive or overly inquisitive; the interview was a consequence of what he considered his duty. His job as manager of the ashram was designing for pilgrims what he called "The most auspicious visit to the Mother's birth."

This was Ganapati-ji, the ashram's senior saddhu and Lal Baba's anointed successor. He was a monarchical 30-something, dressed in a thick, patterned blanket coat, a make-shift turban and shiny black and gold pointy-toed Rajastani shoes. His demeanour and attire were more of an off-season courtier than a high altitude ascetic, but there could be no doubt of his love for his guru and his commitment to the ashram.

Ganapati spoke fair English and soon revealed that he held a masters degree in political science. His attraction to the ascetic life had been initiated by a dissatisfaction with the "crude, pointless" world he had faced upon graduation. He had opted for a simpler course, beyond the subcontinental rat race, a path he believed would, in the long run, yield greater benefits.

As he talked it became obvious that his way to bliss was a path defined by his guru and the teachings of the ancient Indian scriptures, the Vedas. It was a way of power and the word "power," I soon discovered, cropped up with disturbing frequency in our discussions. Ganapati-ji wanted the strength of his guru and of the deities from which that power was derived.

The Ganga was an integral part of his quest for the pure and the strong. For Indians the river is as incorruptible as a mother's love and, even in youth, powerful enough to toss glacial boulders to its banks like beach pebbles.

Ganapati added, "It is pure, here at Gaumukh this is obvious, but even farther downstream, when pilgrims take it to South India for religious purposes, it does not stagnate."

Gangotri is the first settlement on the river's descent. It is an ad hoc hamlet pieced together around the temple that lends the village its name. In the pilgrimage or Yatra season, from May to October, the ashrams and guest houses scattered around the village are overflowing with the faithful. But I arrived well into winter and was barely noticed by the skeleton crews that had been left behind. I wandered the empty, refuse-littered streets looking for a room and was eventually taken in by Baba Bal Bharati of the Gaurikund ashram.

The Baba was a middle-aged, dreadlocked saddhu with yellowing eyes and teeth to match. His natty dreads reached down to his bum and were matched frontally by a navel-length beard. He wore multicolored robes that were a jigsaw puzzle of patches. Bal Bharati had a distant, disconcerting air and the disarming ability of never blinking.

The Baba was a serious Hindu practitioner whose days were absorbed in meditation and ritual. In the ashram's courtyard he showed me his preferred place of worship, the ashram's shrine to the god Shiva, one of the three greatest Hindu dieties. It was a sunless concrete bunker the focus of which was the lingam, an abstract stone representation of Shiva's male power. From the base of the stone extended the yoni, the image of his wife Parvati, and the image of female energy. In that sanctum, before the fusion of male and female, the saddhu sat crosslegged, deep in meditation hour after hour, reciting his mantras and repeating his rituals while five meters away the rushing Ganga drowned his words in fluid noise.

When not practicing, much of Baba Bal's time was spent in his ashram room. It was a tiny four-walled cell of aromatic deodar cedar that during the winter was dark and damp even at noon. Aids to his contemplation adorned the walls: gaudily printed posters of Shiva, the embodiment of power, Lakshmi, the goddess of wealth, and Ganesh, Shiva's elephant-headed son. The lithographs, now yellowing with age, still bore the names of the companies that had sponsored their printing: Dada Tractor Parts, Natraj Pharmaceuticals, and Mukeesh Paints "...BECAUSE WE WANT YOU BRIGHT, BRIGHT, BRIGHT." In India religion is a business.

The ashram was wrapped along the southern shoulder of the river. At Gangotri the gently sloping banks that characterize the Ganga at Gaumukh disappear; the water abruptly ceases its easy downward meander and for ten kilometers cuts a steep course through solid rock. Here the Ganga transforms from an impatient child to a wildly thrashing Amazon and rips a direct path through strangely slick sandstone. The gorge is up to sixty meters deep and its walls, infinitely cut with glimmering nodes and subtle recesses, become the canvas of her true artistry. The canyon is an ever-changing mosaic paying homage to her creative drive.

The beauty of the gorge is in its permutability; light transforms it. That day, as the sun made its way above the high ridges, the caverns were lit by a soft, refracted light. The river metamorphosed, transforming again from a tempestuous damsel to an alluring nymph. In the glow of that golden hollow was a glimpse at her countless faces, her ability to be something to everyone.

Gaurikund means the cave of Gauri, another of Shiva's many titles, and the Gaurikund ashram derives its name from the neatly carved pool that lies, recessed in the river's northern cliff, directly opposite the temple. For most of the year it is underwater, but with the winter's diminished flow it sits becalmed just above the water's frantic hydraulics. It is a piece of serenity in a storm of mist and foam. For me, with the late autumn leaves floating on its surface adding form and offsetting its unfathomable blackness, it was a brushstroke of perfection.

I stood alone, mesmerized by it, a contemplation that was eventually interrupted by an elbow in my ribs. The motion was accompanied by the smell of woodsmoke and body grease. Beside me was Baba Bal, smiling like a golden-toothed lion. He too was staring at the Gaurikund, and gently, without looking at me, he said, "That is me — peaceful."

The way from Gangotri to Lanka is a vision of the old Himalayas, the mountains of Kipling and Kim. The road winds through thick deodar woods, long-needled giants rising from an uncluttered forest floor. The trees created jagged outlines, emerald baroque frames for the ever-changing mountainscapes to the rear. Their scent was sharp and sweet, a smell that permeated my clothes and brought to me images of tricksters in green.

Lanka itself is barely a village, more an odd assortment of tin shacks scattered over the west side of the Jadh Ganga, one of the mother flow's first major tributaries. Before the bridge, the highest suspension construction in India, was built in 1986 it was the last stop for pilgrim vehicles and the staging ground for the trek farther up to Gangotri.

At one point some intrepid entrepreneurs manually transported a disassembled bus down and across the gorge. Then, upon its reassembly, they charged the elderly and infirm exorbitant prices to motor the last ten kilometers to the temple. Some may have called it highway robbery, but on the subcontinent pilgrimage is accepted to have its hidden costs.

In the village I had tea with Chattor Singh, the chowkidar, or caretaker, of the deserted tourist lodge. We had walked together a few days before on my way up to the source from Dharali, the last stop on the off-season bus route. Chattor was ancient, cross-eyed, thin-shouldered and, because of one leg being shorter than the other, he walked with the jerky, mechanical motion of a wind-up soldier. Yet for all his physical faults I had been surprised by his ability to direct discussion at the tea stalls we'd stopped at along the way.

He was a person well accepted within his community, a simple, straightforward man. His deformities had pushed him to the edge of society but had consequently provided him with the space needed to view that same community with discrimination.

Talk over tea centered on his solitary confinement at the guest house. For the six months of winter he was alone and, other than a biweekly return for fresh supplies, was unable to reach his village, Gangnani, forty kilometers away.

He is one of the few Indians I've ever met with no fear of being alone. For him it was a time to think, and although the Hindu gods offered him a dash of spiritual security, it was the river that provided his true solace. At Lanka the sound of it reverberated through the woods, adding to the penetrating winter peace of the place, mingling with the wind, brushing the conifers' needles and bringing with it the smells of snow and smoke. Chattor summed it up by saying, "I am happy when Ganga is here, it is the sound of my past, it follows me from my village, it is my history."

To the faithful this sound is the resonance of nature, the report of that natural law that Eastern philosophies call Dharma, a vibration that has been recreated in Buddhism and Hinduism as the mantric syllable OM. OM is the echo of life and Lanka in December pulsated with its rythmn.

Near Harsil the river exits its gorge and the bed widens. Ahead the peak of Banderpaunch was dulled by an atmosphere thick with river mist and wind-blown silt. Past Harsil the river performs a ninety degree swing to the south moving finally in the direction of its outlet, the Bay of Bengal.

One of the first villages of the new direction is Gangnani, the winter home for many of Gangotri's holy men. They are drawn there by its more temperate climate and the 30°C springs that emanate from the hillside and gather in an ancient pond carved in stone.

I went in search of the springs and discovered the pool crammed with saddhus relaxing in the caress of the mother's warmth. The sulfuric steam mingled with the tart, sugary aroma of hashish, the Shivite saddhus' drug of choice. The ascetics lined the granite pond, only their heads breaking the surface, their snake-like dreadlocks surrounding them like starbursts. In the steam and fading light it looked as if the water was alive with stoic spiders.

Farther on at Maneri the Ganges' waters are stilled. There, stretching across the river, is the Bheli hydroelectric dam. To its south the water bursts from the wall with orgiastic fury, but on its north side the Ganga is becalmed, a stagnant lake stalled by a flat line of concrete.

Strangely, the eight billion rupee powerhouse is the government's best attempt at bringing art and engineering together, as the dam, a boring strip of cement set against pristine forest, has been painted in neon shades of pink, yellow and blue.

Unfortunately it is a deconstructionist failure because in India such bright colors are more associated with advertising hardsell than high art.

You cannot look at the dam without trying to unearth some subliminal marketing for shampoo, tea, or scotch.

But the most depressing part about the damming of the holy river is the sorrily sporadic output of the power plant. The generators only worked for ten months in 1986 before quartzite in the water caused serious damage to the turbines and brought them to a grinding halt. Since then constant repairs have absorbed more than the initial construction costs. The rationalists blame faulty engineering, but the faithful look at the project as pure folly, saying that the dam's misfortunes are a consequence of Ganga-mai's wrath, her anger at being confined by earthly restraints.

The bus from Maneri to Uttarkashi was typical of those in the mountains, a peeling aluminum skin over a steel and wood frame, all bolted onto a chassis suspended above four bald-treaded tires. It was a vehicle that, through the many holes in the floorboards and the headache inducing suspension, kept you in constant contact with the area's abysmally constructed roads. But the bus to Uttarkashi had been a silent one. The homespun mountain folk had been caught in thoughts of the world outside the shaking corpse of the old bus.

At Dinchan we'd stopped to let passengers disembark and the man sitting beside me had jumped out the door to help his pregnant sister off the bus. He held her hand as she stepped daintily down the rotten stairs. Then, from above, something large and square had fallen off the roof. Its edge caught his skull with a sickening thud and in slow motion he'd dropped to the ground.

Someone had accidently dropped a 30 kilogram sheet metal chest off the luggage rack and now it lay like a smoking gun by the man's side. Everyone was staring at it.

His sister immediately let out a wail of such piercing intensity that we were all pulled back to reality. Images of mothers hanging over contorted victims of war flashed in my mind. People scrambled out and surrounded the body. I could see the man's eyeballs flickering beneath the closed skin of his eyelids and his left foot twitched involuntarily.

The hushed bus had exploded into a cloud of noise: women screamed, men shouted orders, and a baby behind me cried and cried. A group of men dragged the limp body back on board the vehicle and the driver was instructed to get to the nearest hospital as fast as possible. The bus carreened along the road, swaying like a sailboat in heavy winds.

The body lay immobile on the dirty floor to my left. The foot had stopped twitching. The sister was still screaming and slapping her brother on the cheek. But there were no signs of consciousness. From one of his ears blood was starting to ooze. Scarlet red and viscous, it formed a convex pool tight into his close-shaven skull.

Within fifteen minutes we were at a hospital. It was an ominous concrete block, its sandy yellow exterior stained by monsoon rain. The body was shouldered by four men into the lobby. Two of the bearers returned within minutes shaking their heads. The bus pulled away and the bad news spread like a foul smelling odor — his pulse had disappeared.

It was my first personal encounter with death in India and I couldn't help but think that soon the body would join the river. The man's remains would become another memory in the Ganga's continuum.

I was now in Uttarkashi, a city that epitomizes the subcontinent's juxtaposition of the sacred and the profane. The town's movie halls revel in the gyrating hips and seductive lyrics of the latest Hindi blockbusters, the main bazaar advertises a "SEX AND V.D. CLINIC ... CLEAN, SAFE, FAST," and its magazine shops stock the latest Bombay soft-core porn.

But Uttarkashi is also one of India's most sacred cities, a community possessing a mythological history that can be traced back for millennia. Its name literally means "northern city of light" and the northerly approach to the town is lined with ashrams filled with wintering saddhus. The town's reputation is enhanced by the fact that it is the stopover point for pilgrims going to the Ganga's source. Here they rest overnight and transfer buses for the last leg of their journey to Gangotri.

At dawn I went to visit the Viswanath temple, the most famous of Uttarkashi's shrines. It consists of two sanctums set within a brick-floored courtyard, and both were clean and bustling with worshippers. The first contained a sacred Trishul, the six meter trident representing the three primary gods of the religion: Brahma, the creator, Vishnu, the perpetuator, and Shiva, the destroyer. One reason for Ganga's all-pervasive popularity is because her appearance on earth is associated with all three of these gods.

The second of the Viswanath shrines is a spotless marble walled room containing an awe-inspiring lingam. The uncarved stone block, shaped like a collosal, elongated egg, was attended to by doting priests and fawned upon by the faithful. It was draped in dozens of fresh flower garlands and glistened from its morning wash.

The pujari, the master of ritual at any Hindu holy site, told me that only Ganga water could be used to clean the icon. In his words, "Only the purest can cleanse the pure." So stainless is the association of the lingam and the Ganga that the bathing water is collected and distributed to the congregation. It is an ambrosia that, having been in contact with both gods, doubles its potential power.

The next day before sunrise I left Uttarkashi for Tehri, and as we crossed the ridge to the south, I looked back to see the mountains on either side of town cradling a crescent moon. The night sky was illuminated from below by the rays of the still cold sun. The pale chilly glow created a graded horizon moving subtly from silver to black. It was true northern light.

The bus had lost its suspension long before the town of Tehri, but the gouged track we were travelling on did nothing to help the archaic vehicle or its discomforted passengers.

After the peaceful memories of the land farther upstream the lower Bhagriath valley was a shock. There, with the hot, blurred sun high overhead, Tehri looked more like a scene from *Dante's Inferno* than the historical capital of the Garwahl Himalaya. Dust clouds swirled like banshees down the valley floor, obliterating the hillsides, lending a hazy halo to the sun and forcing pedestrians to bundle up like desert nomads.

Dust, I was to discover, was Tehri's trademark. It permeated everything, from the food you ate with a sandy crunch, to the mica layer that glittered on everything, stationary or mobile. Dust was the aftereffect of events that had brought Tehri into the international spotlight.

Tehri, or more exactly the Ganga at Tehri, is to be home to one of the five highest dams in the world. The 260 meter earth and rock fill behemoth will create a lake seventeen kilometers long and displace 15,000 families, including the 12,000 residents of Tehri town itself. The result will be 1,000 megawatts of electricity generated for the power hungry cities of the Gangeatic plain.

The dam was being planned as far back as 1963, but even today the construction appears barely underway. Initial cost estimates were exceeded decades ago and the project has absorbed 250 billion rupees of the struggling nation's reserves. It is the prototype of the third world money pit, but the black comedy of it is that such a project should never have been started.

The Tehri dam lies on one of the most active fault lines in the world. Eight major tremors of a magnitude of 7.5 or more have occurred along the Himal front since the Assam earthquake of 1897. A quake of that scale would almost certainly rupture the dam and from it would burst 2.62 million acre feet of water. The downstream cities of Rishikesh and Haridwar would be washed away within minutes, tens of millions of people would be affected, and the entire length of the Ganga would be changed forever. The Tehri dam is not just a symptom of a bureaucracy that believes in its own infallibility but of an entire nation willing to turn its back on history.

Tehri town has been the whipping boy for a half dozen national administrations over the past thirty years. The town is now a derelict;

everything about it suggests temporariness, and neglect hangs over it like a cloud. The residents have little desire to repair buildings or an infrastructure that will eventually lie under 250 meters of water. The mood extends to the people themselves, for impermanence breeds insecurity, and they are homeless even before their homes are taken.

Yet along the river's edges a minor building boom is taking place. The banks are dotted with oddly angled shacks that look more like the leftovers from an archaic army camp than the houses they are disguised as. The huts will be claimed as homes by those willing to use "the system" as it is using them, and the government will be forced to compensate them for the loss of these "family estates." Maybe this is a gesture of Ganga-mai's generosity in the late twentieth century.

At the guest house in Tehri, a trembling wooden structure that creaked in protest to my slightest movement, I was accosted by the peon. He was a thin, hawk-nosed man whose right eye was in the final stages of glaucoma, an abnormality that caused him to put my every move under double scrutiny.

As I brought out my passport to sign the guest book, his one good eye lit up. He clutched at his breast pocket and retrieved his own Indian passport along with a worn, crumpled letter from his local member of parliament. With this he forgot that I was in the process of registering and began repeating, over and over again, how he also owned a "passaporta." It was as if the word held some magical powers for him. To me it was a sad display of false security. I doubted the man would ever travel outside his country. I took his overzealous possesion of national papers as a sign of the Tehri-ites frantic desire to find a way out of a land that would soon cease to exist.

The next day I crossed the shaky, steel girder bridge over the Ganga. Below it, on the right bank, is the blue clapboard shack that is the ashram of Sunderlal Bahaguna. There, caught between the roar of the river and the raucous clap of the traffic, lives the most dedicated activist in the struggle to halt the dam's construction. It is from that 40-square-meter hut, constructed from the driftwood brought down by the river, that the most consistent opposition to the dam originates.

When I arrived Bahaguna-ji was observing the vow of silence he keeps from nine to five every day, so his disciple, Tenzin, showed me around the ashram.

Off in the background, like yellow ants in a grimy fog, Caterpillar tractors moved earth at the base of the infant dam. This was the provenance of the gritty clouds that shadowed the valley. Gray was the predominant color, for the crushed rock rose from the valley floor and took on a life of its own.

The foreground of this apocalyptic scene was absorbed by a yawning black hole, a massive gateway carved into solid rock, through which the river disappeared. It was water being eaten by the earth. This was the diversion tunnel, the channel that altered the flow of water and permitted work to take place on the river bed. To me it looked as if the river was entering a dark age. As the water departed the world of light it snarled and roared, piling wooden debris at the entrance, trying incessantly to dam the work of the dammers.

At five o'clock Bahaguna-ji ended his silence and the group — his wife, three of his colleagues, himself and I — moved to a stone ledge overlooking the river. There he led us through a series of simple meditations and prayers on Ganga-mai.

Sunderlal Bahaguna looks more like an esoteric holy man than an environmental activist. His long hair and beard are equal in length and as white as new snow. He dresses in homespun traditional clothes and adds a pensive, premeditated air to everything he does. His face speaks of someone content with life and his large, clear eyes are those of a man of purpose. But on the day I was there he appeared tired, his legendary energy was sapped, and as I questioned him about his "Stop the Dam" movement, the reasons for his fatigue became clear.

Bahaguna had been living at the construction site for six years. Early on when the people realized how the barrage would disrupt their lives they had mobilized, but as time wore on the protesters had been beaten, bribed and bought into silence. Now all that was left of an organization that had originally numbered in the thousands were a few dozen loyal supporters. The rest had been hoodwinked by what Bahaguna called the "Quick Fix Religion," a doctrine where the dollar is God, the engineers the high priests, and the dam its greatest temple. Bahaguna sighed when he told me how in India music videos and fast cars were triumphing over deep thought and the considerations for the future. His campaign was losing ground to Coca-Cola and TV.

But Bahaguna-ji's biggest concern was not the river, for he considered the Ganga larger than his movement or any dam consortium. More on his mind was the plight of the people affected by the project. The residents of the Tehri-Garwahl would be exiled; for the lucky their new homes would be thirty-five kilometers away in New Tehri, the government's idea of a mountain utopia. But that new improved Tehri was filled with leaking, cheaply constructed cinderblock houses, an urban planning nightmare superimposed on the deforested Himalaya.

The less fortunate would be forced down onto the plains. There, without access to their land, the legendary "tough as nails" Garwahli hill people would be consumed in India's mammoth urban melting pots. They would have no choice but to join the doomed millions flocking to Delhi and Bombay. There, all they could look forward to would be debt, alienation, and a lack of self-respect. The Garwahli's identity and self-sustainibility would be lost with their land.

I asked Bahaguna's group about the government's grandiose reimbursement schemes. They laughed, and told me how the victims of the system's first major dam project back in the '50s had finally received their compensation — last year.

The prospects for Tehri and Bahaguna's group looked bleak. It was depressing to probe deeper into a cause that was so obviously for the good but had been so expertly neutered by the forces it opposed.

I asked Bahaguna the inevitable, what he thought the chances were of stopping the dam. He raised his eyes to mine and told me how his group would fight until the last day of construction. But now, he added, what they were fighting was not so much the Tehri dam but the dozens of future Himalayan high dams that the government had planned. The organization was alive at this point as much as an example as a viable opposition.

Bahaguna-ji said, "You know, I consider myself and my colleagues to be candles in the night. My friend, do you know the difference between a candle and an electric bulb? A bulb is unable to ignite even one of its compatriots, whereas a candle can light thousands of them."

Darkness was upon us. In the distance the Caterpillars rumbled through the night and arc lights flashed through the dust storms like the evil eyes of Big Brother. Sunderlal apologized that I could not stay at the ashram, telling me, "Just above us, guards from the dam authority monitor us twenty-four hours a day. The government wants to frame me as the agent of foreign powers, so as to send me off to jail again. Therefore, for both our benefits, it would be better if you stayed in town."

With my eyes to the ground I recrossed the swaying girder bridge back into the bony wasteland of Tehri town.

The next day I was back on the road. My next stop was Devprayag, the meeting place of the Bhagriath and its sister stream, the Alkananda. It's here, for cartographical purposes at least, that the river becomes the Ganga.

In legend Ganga-mai had 108 sources and 108 outlets, 108 being the most auspicious number in Hinduism, but the two major tributaries are those that merge at Devprayag. The Alkananda starts to the northeast, close to Tibet. Like the Bhagriath it too passes close to one of the four great Himalayan pilgrimage sites, Badrinath, and it, as well, has an inexhaustible mythology connected to it. Some scholars have argued that the Alkananda is the truest source of the mother flow, but through the force of historical teachers, primarily the great eighth-century Hindu reformer Shankaracarya, it was determined that Gaumukh would have the honor of being the earthly genesis of the Ganga.

I stumbled off a sardine-packed bus and crossed the taut suspension bridge that spanned the river. Along its lines a horde of monkeys eyed me sideways while continuing with their work — picking nits from a neighbor's hair, nuzzling a young one or strutting like macho tightrope walkers along the steel lines. On the opposite bank I followed a maze of tight alleys and found myself descending a set of winding, solid stone stairs to the point marking the confluence.

The two rivers were almost the same color, a turbid, thick, blue-brown. Like two long lost friends they roared and splashed to their point of connection. But out in midstream, at the point of their embrace, all was calm, just a soft rippling, no shouting or calling of names, only the soft whispers of two loved ones.

In the water two people dressed in the thin, white cotton vestments of upper-caste brahmins were religiously bathing. Both were saying mantras and raising water in cupped hands over their heads; the blessings dropped to the flow and were absorbed in the river. The current created rushing, rippling vortexes behind their thin legs, pulling the loose ends of their robes downstream like wet bandages. I was impressed by their steady stance because in the turbulence at the confluence only the strong dare to pray.

I walked a short distance back up the hill to the town's main temple, a beautiful carved granite Garwahli-style shrine, shaded by trees and surrounded by a spotless courtyard. Inside were statues of Ram and Sita, the main characters of the Hindu Ramayana epic.

The resident priest approached and tried to explain some of the shrine's history, but his English failed him and he introduced me to Swami Sachiananda. He was a young man with a wide face and a huge grin. He had the dark Dravidian features of a South Indian and wore only the simplest ochre robes and a light brown shawl.

He led me outside into the evening twilight where we sat on a low wall and listened to the river. He talked about the history of the temple and Devprayag and had soon moved on to an explanation of

Hindu Vedanta philosophy. The Swami was a natural teacher and led the way through the discussion by offering more questions than answers.

Darkness fell and the conversation returned to more worldly matters. He had, at one time, been a lecturer in chemistry, and so had the enviable ability to pose his spiritual theses within a scientifically rational framework. But institutional duties had gotten in the way of his practice, so he had departed academia. His chosen way was an unquantifiable quest. As he told me, "Poverty is sufferable, ignorance is not." Money was of no consequence to Sachiananda; he lived as a beggar on twenty dollars a month in a shack across the river that he had helped build. As he said, "You can add zeroes to the right of 1 and increase its value infinitely. But first you must know the one. Until then all the zeros are exactly that, zero."

The moon was up and a breeze following the river's path down from the mountains added a subtle chill to the air. It was time to leave, but upon his invitation, I agreed to visit the swami early the next day.

The following morning the sun was bright and warm. The long, neatly cut shadows made even the dull, denuded hills leading up from the sparkling river look exceptional. Back across the suspension bridge I found Swami Sachiananda in a yoga position outside his hut. He was repeating mantras and enjoying the day's heat. As I arrived he jumped to his feet with astonishing dexterity and with a Cheshire cat smile welcomed me to his humble home.

Before we could continue our conversation from the day before the swami insisted that we pay our respects to his next door neighbor whom he described as an accomplished teacher. Swami Om Giri, it turned out, was also a veteran of the British Indian army's World War Two campaigns so, by my reckoning, he was well into his seventies. Yet when I saw him outside his hut, cross-legged and reciting verses from the Ramayana, he could easily have passed for a man in his fifties. His only submission to age was the thick reading glasses that perched precariously at the end of his nose.

Swami Sachiananda introduced us. Om Giri-ji looked up, his long mane of silvery hair almost touching the ground, and with a distinct British accent said, "Welcome, very nice to meet you." With that he closed his ancient, clothbound book, tucked his thumb between the covers to mark his place, rose, and walked straight back into his hut. It appeared that Swami Om Giri wasn't overly excited to meet me. Sachiananda-ji looked on with his boyish eyes dancing. He laughed, content that his introductory duties were complete, and we returned to his hut.

The swami's two meter by two meter shack was a spartanly simple concrete box. The room was deceptively cozy. The pale blue walls had an imperceptible depth, for their matte tone smoothed out the stones' roughness and brought the sky inside. Niches in the thick walls held images of Lord Krishna, an incarnation of Vishnu and the focus of devotion for hundreds of millions of Hindus. Other recesses were crammed with religious texts in seven languages and still other nooks and crannies contained his few eating and writing utensils. His abode was a teaching in itself, simple possessions assembled in a way that showed a complete knowledge of the space.

I asked about the created modesty of his home and the swami talked about how every object radiated a particular energy, good or bad, and that these can disrupt or assist the body's own ability to reach a state of equilibrium. Thus he kept possessions and their display to a minimum and, in fact, performed his meditations in the empty hut next door.

The river, ten meters down the bank, was a constant presence in the cabin, its flow visible through two small, unglazed windows set low in the front wall. The water sound wound easily around the walls, giving the space a sonic depth while simultaneously generating a warm hum. The hut was a receptacle for the river's ever-present mantra.

We talked for a few hours but eventually returned to the concept of radiant energy and how it applied to the most conspicuous object in our midst, the river. Sachiananda-ji explained how the Ganga has been a place of worship since time immemorial. The river has had a symbiotic relationship with all the enlightened individuals who have practiced along it. For those able to appreciate it, said the swami, the river is an unlimited source of spiritual energy. The Ganga for him was a colossal broadcasting system, a liquid radio station transmitting a non-stop program on nirvana. In his words, "The faithful's job is to simply tune mind and body to the correct channel." Then the river will always be there, washing over them, cleansing, purifying, and bringing them wholeness.

The Swami finished his sentence, looked down at the river, laughed and said, "You know, maybe one of the best parts of this radio is that it needs no batteries."

The road below Devprayag follows the general course of the river, but to do this the motorway climbs and descends with terrifying frequency. In the depths of the descents the hills surround you and become a jade bowl holding in a washed blue sky. But at their crests the Ganga appears far below, a teal brown snake winding its way through a mottled green gorge.

The tragic absence of trees in the valley has left the slopes scarred by the monsoon's violent rains. Without a matrix of root systems to hold and absorb the precipitation the heavy rains of summer simply wash over the slopes, carrying away the precious top soils needed to nurture the much needed forest.

There was a welcome respite from this stark deficiency as I drew closer to the pilgrimage center of Rishikesh. Here the forest crept down to the river and its branches dipped their delicate fronds into the sacred flow.

I decided to make a stop twenty kilometers north of the town at the holy cave of Vashist Goofa. I climbed down from the road and discovered, caught between the river and a simple ashram, a cliff face of candle-wax smooth stone painted glossy white. Set into the base of the rock wall was a crooked indigo door, behind which was the grotto. Fifty meters away were a set of concrete blockhouses, the quarters of the swamis, the teachers at the monastery, and visiting saddhus.

I rounded the buildings and walked to the river on a path of flat, precariously balanced stones. The flow was bordered on each bank by a dense forest of overhanging branches. They were gnarled, large leafed trees of the kind that become home to monkeys, snakes and flocks of parrots. The Ganga ran smooth and fast over a bed of multicolored boulders clearly visible through water tinted the green of antique bottles. It was an exotic childhood dreamscape and I sank back onto my haunches to appreciate it more.

But my daydream didn't last for long. In a few minutes I was hearing shouts and screams from afar. I thought at first there had been an accident up on the road, but as the noise grew louder I saw, edging around the upstream bend, two huge yellow and gray inflatable rafts festooned with Coca-Cola logos. It looked as if all out war had been declared between the two. Slapping paddles sent cascades of water back and forth.

The rafts moved quickly, drawn by the current, spinning gracefully like ice dancers without music. They drew parallel and half the crews turned to face me and shouted in unison, "BONJOUR!" After the quietude of the ashram it was a shock and I delayed in adding even a smile and a wave. Then with subsiding fanfare the Gallic holiday-adventurers disappeared around the lower bend. I was left alone again with the far-off screech of monkeys and the silent flow of the jungle Ganga.

I went back to the cave and there found two swamis and a pair of lay practitioners chanting mantras in an alcove before the cavern. The rounded syllables echoed smoothly off the cliff walls and rolled on down to the river. It was an infectious sound and I joined the group.

After a steady hour of prayers the group stood and proceeded into a cacaphonic ringing of bells and gongs. The strange symphony brought a small black and white dog that had lain peacefully on one of the swami's laps to its feet and it accompanied us by howling at the top of its lungs. The dog was the mascot of the ashram. One of the saddhus told me it had come to the cave as a puppy, skinny, sick and on the edge of death. It would take no food and was too weak to go anywhere else. On its third day at the ashram the saddhu had taken the dying animal to the prayer session in front of the cave and with the final beating of the gongs it had suddenly leapt up, the hair on its neck standing on end, and joined in the precussion chorus. The dog had made a miraculous recovery and since then had never missed a cave side prayer gathering.

After the prayers I was permitted into the cave. Through the little indigo door was a low-ceilinged vestibule. There I took off my shoes. The floor was icy cold and even through my woolen socks it sent shivers up my spine, a reminder that possibly I was in the presence of something powerful. I ducked through the opening into the main cave and the sunlight was lost.

It was imperceptibly black except for a tiny oil lamp burning in a far niche. I leaned back against the wall and felt the chill seep into my torso. As my eyes adjusted I could see that the lamp was illuminating a small brass statue. Above it hung a bowl of water suspended from the roof by three chains. The water, undoubtedly that of the Ganga, dripped like a slow metronome on the figure, constantly cleaning it and leaving it with a shimmering liquid skin. The cave's enclosed acoustics held each drip's subtle slap and the notes reeled around the walls, almost until the next purifying drop was released. I clung to the sound. It was an aural meditation on continuity.

Eventually a village man entered the darkness. Unaware of me he reverentially approached the statue while muttering mantras under his breath. He dropped to the ground before it, clasped his palms in prayer, laid his forehead to the floor and, after some time, lowered his hands to the base of the statue. There he left an offering, rose to his feet and departed. From my seat in the rear I could see in the flickering light of the oil lamp that his gift had been a single, freshly plucked, marigold.

Back outside in the bright light I was able to talk to Swami Sadhananda, a vigorous, silver-haired septarian who wore his steel-rimmed reading glasses on top of his head like a bicycle racer. He told me how he considered the cave one of the two most powerful places in India.

Vashist Goofa was named for the head tutor of Lord Ram, the hero of the the Ramayana epic. Guru Vashist had used the cave for many years as a spiritual retreat and I asked the Swami why the teacher would have chosen this spot as his refuge. His answer lay with the river.

He reminded me that for Hindus this world is one of trial and tribulation; life is full of suffering and calm is something that must be achieved through practice. The Ganga has the power to show people what their practice can lead to. In his words, "There is a door in us all that leads to peace, but to open it we need a key. For many, including Guru Vashist, that key is the Ganga."

Just above Rishikesh in the town of Laksman Jhula I took a room that overlooked the impressive suspension bridge that connects the two halves of the community. The bridge was a galvanized, Lilliputian Golden Gate, large enough to facilitate two-way pedestrian traffic yet not quite wide enough to accommodate a car. This was the Ganga's first crossing on the plains and one of her last mountain memories. The midday winds coming south out of the mountains buffeted the bridge and for the pedestrians were a reminder of the goddess's tempestuous youth.

In the afternoon I made my way to Shanti-mai's ashram on the west bank. Shanti-mai is an American Hindu teacher whose years of practice have led many to believe that she has attained a state of enlightenment. She now divides her time between Rishikesh and the States, transferring her message to a growing congregation.

As I passed through the compound's iron gates I asked an ancient Indian baba where the daily gathering was taking place. Sporting a prodigious Father Christmas beard, an impish grin, and a pair of Italian prescription glasses the old man was memorable. He pointed me in the direction of a fiftyish Caucasian woman, who in turn directed me to a large, box-shaped prayer room.

It was a simple, square concrete structure, with three walls of windows facing the mountains. Around it an encircling walkway, deeply worn with the footprints of the circumambulating faithful, displayed the devotion of Shanti-mai's following. I entered and took a seat inconspicuously to the rear.

The room was filled with westerners in all shapes, sizes and shades. The mantra chanting began a little hesitantly, but soon the syllables gained an undulating cadence and I fell into their repetitive simplicity. Soon after the rythmn was found a woman walked in, moved to the front, assumed the lotus position and added her voice to the chorus. Her chanting was exceptional. It added an entirely new range to the occasion — the hard-edged atmosphere of the believers smoothed into a display of heartfelt devotion.

Occasionally she would intersperse her chants with comments like "Softer, don't push it," or "Not so loud, you don't have to shout to be heard." At one point she halted the entire procedure and the crowd stumbled like a stuttering train out of the mantra. "No, no remember," she said gently. "Chant like water trickling down a mountain."

This was Shanti-mai, a 40-something, Californian-looking woman of medium height, solid build, and shimmering blond hair. She wore a rose cream robe that hid her body, but left little doubt that she was a woman. Her skin looked implausibly soft and her eyes smiled as easily as her mouth. Her body language was of a person balanced and confident, and consequently she appeared much younger than her years. It was difficult not to be drawn to her, for she exuded a motherly warmth. In that concrete box she was the focus. It was her voice, deep and beautiful, that had transcended the chanting and brought the group to a higher plane.

After the mantras had ended the assembly rose and led by her walked to an open veranda next door. There on a low dais, his gaze looking out over the river, was her guru, Hanser Maharesh. I sat down with a smile, as he was none other that the sprightly old baba who in the morning had directed me to the prayer room.

The audience with the Maharesh was a "darshan," which in Sanskrit means "to have silent communion with." The disciples sang and meditated while the guru sat quietly and added his spirtual weight to the gathering.

Darshan can be accomplished not just with living masters but with statues, relics or religiously charged aspects of the landscape. The Ganga is the most obvious and potent example of this. It is more than just a metaphor for the mother goddess; for Hindus it is the mother goddess. Almost daily on the river I would see people, standing or sitting silently on the banks, hands pressed together in prayer, quietly appreciating the flow, attempting to capture some of the peace and quietude of the river.

Darshan is a way of sharing a person or object's internal power. With landscape this transmittance occurs just by being there, because it instills a consciousness of the energy around you. But with anthropomorphic objects the focus is always on the eyes. These are the centers through which spiritual energy is transferred.

The group at Hanser Maharesh's darshan was fixated upon his eyes. Their vigorous chanting shook the veranda, but the Maharesh was unfazed and silently he repayed the devotion. The scene around him was louder and more aggresive than that surrounding Shanti-mai. The noise reverbarated around us in crashing waves. The pair had two completely different guru styles — where Shanti-mai had been a subtle shepherdess, the Maharesh was an anchor in a sonic storm.

In the afternoon I returned to the ashram for Shanti-mai's satsang, or question and answer period. It was held in the shade of an ancient shade tree around which a small Zen-like stone garden had been built. A crowd of about fifty westerners had gathered, radiating out from Shanti-mai's seat at the base of the tree like rays of light. The birds and squirrels chirped in the green canopy and the Ganga, seventy meters away, contributed an omnipresent background mantra.

I was impressed by her patient, well put answers, statements delivered with just a touch of comic drama. Eventually I was able to ask the question that had been with me since she had first joined the morning chanting: "What role had the Ganga played in her spiritual experience?" Shanti-mai was almost excited as she answered, "Well . . . *so* much." She explained how the Ganga had become for her an opening, a doorway into the space where she could discover her fullest potential. After this initial statement she halted, took a sip of tea and replaced the cup deliberately on the low wooden table to her right. She had given me a stock answer and I was unimpressed, but then she continued, "Ganga has taught me grace. It has shown me how to move through people and provide for them, to give them what is needed and move on, unattached."

This answer pleasantly shocked me. The Ganga as grace was something so obviously true that it was invisible. To realize it you had to possess that same grace in yourself. Her answer elevated the river to the role of guru and it connected Shanti Mai with the Ganga.

Rishikesh, the next city on the Ganga's path, is the mythological home of the *rishis*, the seven great Vedic sages who went beyond the normal pursuit of knowledge in their quest for the truth. Thus it is one of India's great pilgrimmage sites, and the constant flow of religious tourists has created a flourishing business in the spiritual. Rishikesh has possibly become, thanks to the Beatles and their guru, the Maharishi, the place most associated in western minds with the mysterious east. It has all the elements — learned swamis, crazed saddhus, outlandish devotional art, yogic masters, cave dwelling ascetics, mountain meditators, long-term ashrams, and teachings, literature, and multimedia events in a plethora of languages. It is a smorgasbord of the divine and the main course in its cosmic feast is the river. The Ganga is the backbone of the community, and it flows through this mystic metropolis with a silent speed that makes her seem oblivious to the frantic devotion heaped upon her.

For me, however, Rishikesh was a weak merger of east and west. Like fusion cuisine gone wrong I couldn't quite taste what was supposed to be happening. It wasn't so much disagreeable as mildly confusing, and possibly Rawa Martin was the best example of what I felt.

I met him initially my first night in town. In the darkness, while taking a closer look at a riverside shrine room, I had stumbled upon a pile of rags in the building's outer walkway. The pile had moved, moaned, and from amidst it a dozy head had appeared and greeted me. Startled, I'd stepped back and mumbled a quick greeting, which was replied to in startlingly good English: "Hello, how are you?" I'd told the waking man that I was fine and we set into a long, sleepy conversation.

Rawa Martin pulled himself from his bed of cast-offs and proceeded, unprompted, to divulge his life story. He had, up until six years ago, been an accountant in the government service; this explained his flawless Indo-English. But God had called him in an office borne vision and he had unquestioningly answered by dropping tiresome responsibilities and setting his feet on the spiritual path.

This is a not uncommon occurrence for older Indian men, and it is considered the fourth stage of the traditional Hindu life. Once their families are provided for, and their questions have turned to the religious, it is accepted that they will take the chance to wander the motherland in search of greater answers.

Rawa Martin drifted for five years seeking a geographic location that spoke to him and eventuallly settled upon Rishikesh. Martin, as with everyone in the town for study and practice, had a connection to the Ganga. For him it was living reminder, a divine footnote that the work of the spirit is unceasing. Like the practice of religion it is continual, the waters at the source and at the outlet being different and yet part of the same continuum.

More so, in relation to Rawa Martin, the Ganga is indiscriminate, because like a true mother she makes no distinction between race, religion, sex or caste. This fact hadn't occurred to me until I caught up with Rawa Martin later on the next afternoon, this time in the light of day.

The night before, in the darkness of the shrine, I hadn't been able to see him clearly. His only distinguishing feature was a distinct smell, unfortunately that of human excrement. I smelt him the next day, on a riverside trail north of town, and was surprised to see a man with more facial hair than Karl Marx, dressed in what looked like homespun white sackcloth and handmade knee-length boots of multicolored canvas. On almost every square inch of his clothing he had painted, embroidered or stitched symmetrical red crosses, and around his neck, dangling from a length of heavy fishing line, hung a massive sandalwood crucifix.

Martin had omitted a key element from his tale of the night before: he was not in fact a Hindu ascetic but belonged to the rarest breed of Indian renunciates, the Christian saddhus.

But it got stranger. As we sat in a cave worn out of the golden river sandstone Rawa Martin told me how he believed, wholeheartedly, that he was the second coming of Christ. As a child his parents had mentioned that he wasn't theirs at birth, a statement he interpreted as evidence for immaculate conception. Moreover, he had had strange visions throughout his life, culminating in his direct calling from God six years before, a vision that directed him to commit himself, like Jesus, to relieving the suffering of the masses. Upon this vision he had superimposed a Ghandian sensibility and now believed that his "life was his lesson." He was leading the world to salvation through his own shining example.

His life exceeded fiction. Yet the combination of the man, the religion, the river, the conviction that he felt, and, not least, the country that we were in, made it all feel wildly possible.

While the sound of the river washed through the cave, we broke a stale chapati to partake in the body of Christ, and with that the newest messiah launched into a five minute prayer for my benefit. It was something between Sunday morning TV evangelism and a *Sesame Street* learning song, abrupt, rhythmic and beautiful. I was touched when he told me sincerely that he would pray for my happiness. I couldn't help but feel that he was a genuinely good person.

I gave him twenty rupees for lunch and he trundled on down the road, his big bag of glad rags slung over his shoulder and his cotton moon boots sending up clouds of dust in his wake.

Haridwar is a city not built around the trading prosperity that a river metropolis innately grows upon, but on India's elementary connection to the Ganga. Haridwar is the Ganga's opening to the plains. Here she leaves the confines of the mountains. Here is where she widens and begins her planar meanderings. Here, in the spiritual geography of Hindustan, is where the Mother Goddess achieves maturity.

In the mountains the Ganga is viewed as an adolescent, playful, innocent, but in many ways unfocused and overly emotional. She is pulled downwards as much by the draw of the far ocean as by her own will. In the monsoon her destruction can leave the valleys wondering what is holy about her and in the dry season she trickles past, taunting the population with her seasonal fluctuations.

But after Haridwar a great change takes place — she gives consciously. She deposits the soils she has leached from the mountains, she irrigates the fields of the Hindu heartland and she caresses the faithful who go to her waters. Even when she delivers a destructive reminder it is through the lapping rise of a rainy season flood, slow-burning evidence of her power.

Haridwar is the site of the Goddess's confirmation, a place that can channel her infinite power into a humanly realizable form. It is a space where her devotees' wildest imaginings can become reality. That faith in Haridwar's transcendent geography has made it one the four most sacred cities in India.

The ritual of the sacred bath is the culmination of every pilgrim's long journey. From dawn until dusk the city's bathing areas, or ghats, are packed with those in need of the Mother Goddess's liquid touch. A constant stream of the wet and blessed descend and rise from the swift waters.

But one of the strangest things about the earnest bathing that takes place in Haridwar is that the water that flows by the city is not the "real" Ganges but, in fact, the Grand Ganga Canal. The channel runs from the city almost 250 kilometers to the meeting point of the Ganga and Yamuna rivers at Allahabad. It neatly dissects the earth between the two waterways and irrigates the vast tract of once arid farm land known as the Doab.

The grand canal scheme was envisioned and executed in the 1860s by the British engineer H. Cautley. The thought of tampering with the Goddess initially infuriated the Haridwari priests and a violent opposition evolved around the project. But Cautley, attuned to the fact that in India religion is business as well as duty, turned the tide of opinion by proposing an elaborate set of ghats along the new shoreline in honor of the Gods. The clergy, aware that a consistently flowing river and new space for pilgrim rest houses would bolster their own fortunes, finally gave their consent.

The work, one of the great engineering marvels of the Victorian era, took thirty years to complete and brought tens of thousands of hectares under cultivation. It was the prototype of the great irrigation works that would spread across India in the years after independence.

But in a way it was also a remaking of the original Ganga creation myth. Legend has it that seven thousand years ago in order to relieve his country of a drought, King Bhagriath had carved a channel from Ganga's mountain home to the ocean in order to release her healing waters. Ganga accepted the pathway and flowed to the sea bringing with her a new era of prosperity and happiness to Bhagriath's empire.

I left my guesthouse early and walked the short distance on dew damp streets to the Hari-ki-puri ghat. The air was sharp before the sun's arrival and there was a clean wetness in the air. The Ganga ripped by the walkway's concrete steps fast and clean, noiseless except for the rustling she made around prostrating bodies, iron pillars and thick, rusty safety chains.

The ghat at that early hour was all but empty, populated mainly by the salesmen of religion. In corrugated metal huts shivering hawkers were selling containers for the sacred waters, flower and incense offerings, and tea to ward off the chill. By the water the heavyweights of the spiritual marketplace, the pujaris, had set up shop. The two groups of retailers were distinctly separated along caste lines and they huddled around makeshift fires, warding off winter's grip and waiting for the morning's first customers.

By 6:30 a.m. the bathing areas were teeming. It was a traffic jam of bodies all waiting for their chance to enter the freezing waters. As the pilgrims dropped into the river their movements would become frantic, their dips fast motion soaks like sparrows in a garden bath. There were screams of excitement and whoops of exhiliration. Only the children were wary, and it was the grandparents' job to press them on. They entered hesitatlingly, but once in the flow there was no escape, and they threw themselves to the Goddess's icy embrace.

The sun crept up from behind the Himalayan foothills to the east. The bloodred disk hung over the river, moving out of the surface fog with a languid, confident speed. We were being given a glimpse of the two powers that made life possible, sun and water.

In the rose-tinged light, around the edges of the bathing crowds, ravens soared and swooped, cawing raucously in an attempt to break the focus of the immersed. A single raven took a seat on a pole before me. It stared at me, cocked its head in a quizzical motion and let out a blasting cackle. They were boisterous tricksters, mediums between the worlds, wild messengers checking on the progress of the faithful.

With the slowly rising temperature the night's wet remains turned to vapor and the fog rose to envelope the procession of blanket-cloaked pilgrims. The mist of dreams was replaced with the atmosphere of the divine as they descended for their sleepy meeting with the Goddess.

Later that day, half lost and not concerned, I was wandering Haridwar's dirty, litter-strewn streets when a I heard a voice in properly accented English ask, "Are you OK, sir? Do you need some help?" Expecting to see a uniformed schoolboy, I turned and was instead accosted by a scruffy, bowlegged man riding a bicycle rickshaw. He had three days' growth appearing from under his unwashed face, his clothes had the frayed, unpatched look of remorseless poverty, and his eyes were the same yellow as his alcohol riddled liver. Yet this middle-aged street dweller spoke the language of the Indian upper class.

John David had been educated, on scholarship, at a "good" school in one of the Himalayan hill stations. But after years behind the books he had emerged to find that, in the real world, there were no jobs for him. He was from a poor, landless, converted Christian family and had discovered his career choices blocked at every turn by the labyrinthine obstacles of caste and family. He was bitter and had fallen to drink.

It was with the upper-caste Brahmin, the implementers of the caste system, that he laid the blame for his demise. More-over, when I told him of my interest in the river he accused the same class for what he called "The dissolution of her power." As he said, "Many times I have gone there to pray as a Christian, but I have felt nothing and she gave nothing. There may have been some power there millenniums ago, but it is gone, eaten by greedy pujaris and fat Brahmin."

It was a sad sight, this pathetic, sullen figure sitting slump-backed on his rusty chariot. No doubt, caste had inhibited his advance in life, but I thought his difficulty in appreciating the Ganga had more to do with his inability to overcome resentment.

I couldn't help but feel sorry for him and without asking myself why gave him a ten rupee note, knowing it would be invested in a mid-day bottle of violently inebriating local liquor.

Bhuj Ghat is the closest that the Ganga ventures towards the exploding metropolis of Delhi. I am unaware of any epic relationship between this ghat and the river; its specialness is due simply to its proximity to the creeping, shanty town suburbs of India's capital.

Delhi is not a place that evokes images of Hindu fidelity, and the city has all but forgotten that one of Hindustan's legendary seven sacred rivers flows through its own neighborhoods. To Delhi-ites the Yamuna river is an exclamation mark on the landscape, an obstacle in crossing from east to west. Few ghats have been built along its shores and the last great cremation to grace its banks was that of Mahatama Ghandi, fifty years ago.

Alternately the Ganga is a question mark, somewhere to venture to when queries are to be answered. This explains the constant flow of devotees stepping down from the decrepit looking Delhi Transport Corporation buses, and the lines of shiny new Maruti sedans lining the dirt streets of the village.

I arrived as the sun was setting and was in a rush to find a room. The pilgrim rest houses, or Dharamsalas, had a monopoly on bed space and were charging preposterous rates for an uncovered patch of concrete floor. I crossed back over the highway and found myself in the compound of the state water authority.

There, two mammoth white buffaloes draped in ornately embroidered Rajastani robes sat beneath a tree, chewing cud and letting time pass. Ten meters behind them was the wooden wheeled cart that the buffalo had the responsibility of hauling. In the fading light I could see that the interior of the covered wagon was brimming with a kaleidoscope of colors and textures. The vehicle looked like a magician's trunk on wheels, its contents a mystery that would change with each opening.

After a while I realized that the cart was a stage and the people gathered by the pair of small cooking fires were a troupe of traveling puppeteers. The women all wore long skirts and tight blouses in complex designs of layered fabrics. Their outfits were fantastically embroidered and inset with glittering mirrors, metal filigree and fine rustling chains. Their costumes were as dramatic as their careers.

The men were simpler in white knee-length shirts and baggy trousers, their heads wrapped in turbans of the brightest colored gauze. Each man had the same theatrically huge drooping handlebar moustach hanging from his upper lip.

I moved to a fire closer to the main building. There three men, two in local dress and one in western clothes and thick black-rimmed glasses, sat on their heels appreciating the blaze. The bespectacled man looked up and with a smile said, "You are a tourist. Welcome, there is room for you." With that he offered me a glass of hot milky chai.

The man turned out to be the caretaker of the complex. After our tea he showed me to the water authority's guest room, a dusty, disused apartment with cracked concrete walls and broken furniture. The space had clearly been without guests for more than a few seasons. I was tired and lay down for a nap. The mattress was as soft as a single blanket on solid wood but in my state it didn't matter.

I woke groggily a few hours later to the sound of drums and cymbals. There were flickering lights outside the windows and I pulled back the tattered curtain. Outside, the two campfires had multiplied to a dozen. In the middle of this ring of fire stood the wagon theater, illuminated by a pair of brilliant, white kerosene lamps. To the right a trio of men were warming up on tabla drums and stringed instruments. At each of the fires and around the stage an audience had gathered. The field was alive with shadowy figures moving through the wavering light, ignorant of the discordant rhythm put out by the practicing orchestra.

I dressed and went outside. The drumroll had begun, the show was about to begin, and the audience was moving in its direction. I took a seat on the grass twenty meters from the wagon and its miniature stage curtains opened with a stutter. On the scene above the backboard was a puppet working a field with a tiny hoe. In the background a pale blue sky hung over far-off trees.

The little farmer's arms worked the plow expertly while he sang long, low folk songs from a mouth that was out of proportion to his body. The orchestra gave accompaniment and the little man happily danced through his fields.

47

Then the peasant was visited by a fat man in black who asked for money. The farmer had no cash and was berated loudly by the loanshark, who stole his only possession, the hoe. The userer departed and set off across a river in his boat. In the background, caught between the river and the sky, was Ganga-mai riding her mythical vehicle, the elephant-nosed serpent, Makara.

The Goddess had seen how the fat man had treated the peasant and was not about to let such base behavior go unpunished. A storm broke out over the loanshark's boat and from beneath the waves a clutch of serpents, the water dwelling nagas, rose up and without fanfare hauled the screaming loanshark into the depths. The crowd rose to its feet and cheered raucously for the oppressor's demise.

This set the tone for a set of fifteen-minute performances that saw the same plot repeated. In each a poor man was wronged and the gods rallied to his defence. The audience was gripped by the fairytales, because they offered a three hour escape from the truth of their lives. Maybe it was only a parable of what could be, but it was also a chance to believe in the impossible.

It is close to Bhuj ghat, moreso than at Haridwar, that the geographical change in the Ganga can be appreciated. There the Himalayan foothills are nowere to be seen. There, in the dusky shimmering light of early afternoon, I was able to comprehend the extent to which the river had curbed its pace and widened its path. Once released from her mountain confinement she blossoms, transforming from a rushed adolescent into an exploratory adult. The Goddess stretches outwards, pushing the limits of her fluid form, moving silently into the slips around villages, filling the sluices and channels in brackish swamps, finding backwaters and eddies in which to rest, and silently, persuasively through it all she carves a passage in the direction of her choice.

The river in this planar environment becomes not just an all pervasive sound but an inescapable physical presence. On the plains it is impossible to distance yourself from her. All water leads in her direction.

From the forgotten drip of the municipal tap to the monsoon flood of Bihari tributaries the waters move to the mother. The terrestrial world too is intrinsically tied to her, for all the high ground gazes down upon her, all the fields and wetlands rely on her replenishment. All roads and rails track or intersect her, and the human settlement of the basin has occurred only with her blessing. Ganga-mai is a liquid axis mundi for the 330 million people who drink from her stream and rely on her compassion for their sustenance.

Kanpur is the largest city in India's most populous state. Uttar Pradesh has more people than Germany, Switzerland, Austria, Holland, and the Scandinavian countries combined. It is a state so heavily populated and growing so rapidly that it is almost beyond control. U.P is a state on a whim and a prayer, and Kanpur is the industrial heartland of that commonwealth of chaos.

The industry that has created this metropolis is a throwback to Victorian times. Coal-stained smokestacks and gargantuan brick buildings hum with the sound of steam and diesel. From inside these machine infernos off-shift workers stagger home, their faces colored the same black as the interior of the factories. The city exists on a backbone of fertilizer, leather, steel, and light manufacturing, and the local industries have left their polluted mark on the Ganges. Here for the first time the river is burdened with the results of heavy industry. Rainbow flecked pools of oily residue mar the river's backwaters. Thick, black, streaky effluent gets caught in organic debris from farther upstream, and the smell of the river suddenly takes on a subtle diesel tinge.

I walked to the riverside through disintegrating streets. Through carved archways and past archeological ruins I glimpsed what the city had been. Dilapidated stonework, neglected but impressive even in decay, stepped down to the water, the river's monsoon flood leaving the lower half of the old buildings covered in muddy sand.

Unlike Haridwar, the bathing areas were more a laundry than a place of worship. The slap of wet cloth on stone was the sound of the river in this city. Hundreds of launderers were lined up in the knee-deep water, beating their clothes against wash rocks salvaged from the shoreline architecture.

I walked along the river's north bank and at Sidnath ghat I happened upon the training area of one of the city's wrestling brotherhoods, or archaras. Wrestling in North India is a ritualized, prestigious affair that has as much to do with religion as maschismo. The athletes are associated with the monkey god Hanuman, the muscled primate general of the Ramayana, who through his undying aid to Lord Ram has gained the status of the most helpful deity in the Hindu pantheon. He is the image people approach when in need of assistance, the deity most able to smooth the way for everything from a business deal to a relationship problem. But Hanuman is also a general and a warrior. He is portrayed as having a humanized monkey face on a grandiose body of Arnold Schwarzenegger proportions. He is a simian on steroids.

The wrestlers fashion themselves in the image of their God. They are brawny assistants who through a combination of thought and force can assist their communities. The archaras are as much service organizations as athletic clubs.

When I arrived the men were warming up with calisthenics, ballistic stretching and the swinging of huge maces around their heads. The guru, an ancient with limbs like muscled matchsticks and a thinning head of snowy hair, was in a tiny loincloth and performing contortionistic exercises on the dirt floor. When he saw me he smiled and his charges puffed out their chests. They were happy to have an audience.

Soon the preliminaries were complete and the scrimmages began. The ring was an open-sided sand pit covered with a slate roof and bordered with stone steps for spectators. One wall looked out over the river and there the guru stood observing his proteges, his hands crossed pensively over his hairless chest.

The two contestants, wearing only the tightest of thongs, entered from either side. Their oiled bodies glistened in the wavering light reflected off the Ganga. They slapped their thighs in a precussionary opening. They crouched in preparation, coiled springs of sinewy muscle,

50

and then engaged — limbs twisting, grunts of exertion, the sexual slide of greased skin, the flash of grimaced white teeth against black, black mustaches. Above, the guru nodded, while on the floor bodies became airborne, landing with a thud and a puff of soft sand. One man stood, and his pinned foe rose slowly but without shame, and they both turned to the far wall. There, set into a delicate nook, was a bright orange statue of Hanuman, and to his right two brocade dressed effigies of Lord Ram and his wife Sita, the archetypal Hindu couple. The combatants touched their foreheads and bowed in respect. The wrestling was their worship, their way to keep the institution of India intact.

Eighty-two kilometers east of Kanpur is the ancient capital of Kannauj, which during the eighth century was the premier city of India. It was the center of an empire that spread from Kashmir to Bengal. In its day it was the epitome of culture and religion, a city thriving on the industry brought to it by the river, confident that it was the greatest metropolis for 8,000 kilometers. But, as with all empires, its time came and Kannauj, the golden city, receded into dust. Now it is merely a flying stop for express trains, a curiosity on the tour of forgotten empires.

But for me it was an empire centered on the Ganga, a city existing around the river. So on a sticky hot afternoon I leapt from the Kanpur mail train landing on a platform that was barely a station. Leaving the depot, I headed west on a road alive with thundering transport trucks. I was surprised to find that between the acrid reek of diesel fumes I could smell flowers and herbs, a forest of scents wafting through the olfactory nightmare of highway India. I soon realized that the row of tin shacks lining the road were not selling the standard tea, biscuits or day-old newspapers but were the showrooms of Kannauj's biggest industry — scent. The town is the epicenter of North India's booming aromatic oils business.

I visited each of the huts in turn, savoring the exotic cloud of aromas that increased with each stop. It was a hint of the grandeur that

Kannauj had been, a glimpse of a world that was now only a poorly mapped matrix of earthen mounds.

At the guest house I had chai and dropped into conversation with the man beside me. His name was Prakash Dutta, a local teacher and journalist who, when he discovered my fascination with the river, insisted that I meet with the local surgeon, Dr. Tandoor.

Tandoor, true to the journalist's description, was an encyclopedia of Gangeatic lore. He was a contemplative gentleman in his sixties, an orderly figure in well-pressed pants and a tweed blazer. Below his neatly cropped silver hair his forehead was deeply lined, a sign I interpreted as a life of thought.

We went into the garden of his low, shady bungalow and over tea he reminisced about the river of his childhood. "In those days the river flowed right by the city. There were bathing ghats and every day in the hot season my friends and I would swim. . . . There were fish, plenty of them. I can remember seeing mooshi fish larger than myself . . . The river was worshipped. It was surrounded in ritual. Dozens of people every day were there performing puja. The Ganga was the town's most important temple . . . But like Kannauj itself the river has changed, physically and sociologically."

Today the river has shifted four kilometers north, the ghats are buried under sand and now only the most devoted make the long sunrise trek to her shores.

Dr. Tandoor had thought about the Ganga and the new India. "Two things are eating away at the Hindu's faith in Ganga-mai. One is the incredible increase in pollution and secondly, people are becoming too busy to attend to their spiritual needs." Tandoor believed there was a connection between the increased pollution and the increased pace in people's lives. Modern India was fixated on getting rich quick. According to the doctor, tradition was being sacrificed for an unknown future.

He had painted a dark view of the new India but added a positive postscript by telling me how the Ganga was worshiped even beyond the subcontinent. Doctor Tandoor had travelled widely and related how the most precious gift he could bring to overseas Hindus was a flask of Ganga water. In fact, Hindus in Mauritius had gone as far as to build a miniature Ganga in their own country. It is a massive pool, blessed with water from the physical Ganga and consecrated through prayer. The water has become the focus of Hinduism on the islands. The dead are brought there to be cremated and even the prime minister goes there to pray on the day of Shiva.

Doctor Tandoor had highlighted the same point as Sunderlal Bahaguna, that the physical river may suffer but its spirit is omnipotent.

Bithoor is not an easy place to reach. I arrived there through a combination of train, bus, auto-rickshaw, tempo (a truck-like three-wheeled vehicle), and eventually on foot. Fortunately, the seedy mood that had grown with each leg of my trip was mellowed by a meeting, on the last stretch, with Sunil Dixit. Sunil was a middle-aged, middle manager who appointed himself my personal guide for an exploration of Bithoor.

Unfortunately he spoke no English and his Hindi was accented to the point of misinterpretation. So Sunil quietly towed me around a dozen different shrines and temples in quick succession, encouraging me onwards at each stop with a low, "Aiye, aiye — Come, come."

To him Bithoor was a homely paradise; to me it was a live study in urban entropy. The town was staggeringly over-populated with temples and great houses from a multitude of bygone eras. It was possible to tell how much time had elapsed since the zenith of a particular age by the stage of a structure's decay. Brickwork receded into the river, masonry was chipped and fallen, brass-spired temples hung at odd angles and ghats were eaten by the river's shifting currents.

Yet through this civic derelict a population flourished, for people inhabited the cracks and corners between neighboring ages. The town was an ancient ant hill, an atrophying architectural time line. Bithoor was a living ruin, a real-time museum perpetually caught in that stage before an historic city depopulates. But like a misunderstood old man with tales and legends filling his ancient mind Bithoor was a town of depth and surprises.

Dr. Tandoor had mentioned that in Bithoor there was a silver spike which, according to legend, had been driven into the ground by Brahma, the god of creation, to mark the center to the earth. I decided I had to see "the center of the world" and Sunil brought me to the shrine that housed it.

It was on the main ghat, an open-walled structure just above the flood line of the river. There sat a grinning pujari, his face lined and tanned from years of facing south on the same seat. He was dressed in a tattered sports coat, grubby trousers and the widest smile I'd seen in months.

The old man asked me where I was from, happy to see a pilgrim from some far-off place. I answered, "Canada." His eyes lit up and he laughed uproariously, repeating what he thought he heard, "Ka-Na-Ta-Ka." With that I too broke into a fit of laughter, because the pujari believed that I was from the Indian state of Karnataka. The idea of Canada, for him, was too far physically and psychologically. To him I was a Caucasian pilgrim from India's Dravidian south.

When our fits had subsided I asked him if he would show me the stake that marked the center of the world. I expected him to bring me to one of the larger temples in the vicinity. I was looking for something of gargantuan proportions, an Ashokan pillar, something befitting Brahma, the entity behind genesis. But instead he made a gesture of blessing one step below where he was sitting. There at the upper end of a heart-shaped copper basin was a silver nail the size of a woodwork finishing fastener.

The brahmin smiled ecstatically and I recaptured the wave of our earlier laughter. The old man and Sunil both caught my infectious giggles and we howled at the comedy of the Gods. Brahma's spike to mark the nucleus of the world was smaller than nails that I myself had driven. Brahma was playing a joke on us all, telling us that the center of the world doesn't have to be travelled to, for it is wherever you can sit and laugh with friends.

I left Sunil with much nodding and shaking of hands, and as I was heading back to the bus-stop a car pulled up beside me and the driver offered a lift. I was a little shocked, because hitchhiking in India is not a common practice and when it occurs, it is a fare-based transaction. But I accepted and the driver almost immediately invited me back to his house for lunch. His air of generosity and inquisitiveness made it impossible to refuse.

We entered Bithoor's largest house through a carved sandstone archway two stories high. The driver, it turned out, was Col. P.P. Singh (ret'd.), the hereditary raja of the area. His ancestors were warriors from the Punjab who three hundred years before had been the protectors of one of the great Muslim Maharajah's wives. Legend has it that they saved the life of the Maharani on more than one occasion and the Maharaja, in appreciation of their service, presented them with the land around Bithoor.

The colonel was a relic of the old India. He was a meticulously groomed man with a jawline beard and measured mus-taches. His face had the light sheen of a coconut oil application and the sleeves of his button-down collar shirt were rolled up ready for work.

We sat in his garden, a tropical idyll of trees and flowers, and sipped on lime gins while the colonel directed a bevy of gardeners in the orders of the day. Every once in a while, from the comfort of his deck chair, he would pull a rope attached to the trigger of a shotgun placed high up in the trees. The scene would shake with the cringing blast and from amongst the orchards flocks of crows would take to the sky. The fruit trees were the center of the colonel's business concerns. Spread throughout the area he had an orchard of over a hundred acres and supplied fruit for markets as far away as Delhi and Bombay.

The colonel and his wife only wintered in Bithoor. "Too bloody hot here in the summer!" In the heat they moved up to Simla, the old summer capital of the British Raj.

I enjoyed the colonel immensely. He was hyperactively curious, wanting to know everything about my river journey and adding his own knowledge here and there to my narrative. At one point, while we were talking about the Sepoy Mutiny of 1842 and how the river was its geographic focus, the colonel added how his family had sheltered the infamous Nana Sahib. Nana was the alleged mastermind behind the much heralded Kanpur Massacre of women and children. It was an atrocity that became the catalyst for a complete change in Victorian colonial policy.

When the British had discovered that the Colonel's ancestors were harboring the fugitive they had set their artillery on the family's palace and turned one hundred fifty years of history into Swiss cheese. The shell of the building still loomed a hundred meters to the north of the present house.

The colonel defended Nana Sahib. "Of course I don't think that Nana Sahib actually did it. All fabricated by the authorities. We always had good relationships with those British girls. Why in the hell would we want to kill them?" The colonel was talking in the first person about events that had occurred a century and a half before. History dies hard in India.

I declined the colonel's kind offer to stay the night and he effusively agreed with my decision. "Yes, yes, of course. Got a mission, got to keep going." He left me with a solid slap on the back and two thumbs up. As I recrossed the threshold of his home he shouted after me, "Best of luck, old chap, and watch your back."

Allahabad, the city of Allah, is a strange name for a place so intrinsically a part of Hinduism. Allahabad's Hindu name is Triveni, the three braids. "Three are the holy ladies of the water," says the Rig Veda. This is where the Ganga meets her sister sacred rivers, the Yamuna and the Saraswati.

The Yamuna, whose source is only one set of ridges west of the infant Ganga, has traveled 500 kilometers to meet her sister. The Saraswati has journeyed infinitely farther. It is the invisible river of the underworld, the river of wisdom that comes from the most remote part of all our souls. The Saraswati is the stream of Neptune and Hader. It appears in our realm only at Allahabad, and only to those spiritually awake enough to appreciate its subtle force.

With this image in mind Prayag becomes not just a three- dimensional meeting of rivers but a multidimensional confluence of realities. It is the communion of the Saraswati's netherworldly flow, the Yamuna's earthly stream and the Ganga's celestial river. Triveni is a collision point of space and time.

This is the essence of the Sangam, in Hinduism, the meeting point, the state where our own internal currents converge and become more powerful, more knowledgeable, more compassionate until finally the culmination of those forces leads to the truth, the all-encompassing ocean of wisdom.

I took a bicycle rickshaw the five kilometers from the city to the river's sangam. It was a bumpy ride that traversed a ragged assortment of residential and agricultural areas, the homes taking the higher ground, the fields the lower, river prone zones.

The road ended and ahead was a flat, dusty expanse of land trapped between two rivers. This was the mela, or festival ground, the kilometer long triangular field that annually hosts the winter celebration of Ganga-mai and every twelve years the great Kumbha Mela festival. The Kumbha Melas are the largest gatherings in history. On those astrologically auspicious dates up to 15 million people converge at the sangam in order to pay tribute to the complex organism that is Hinduism.

I started off across the grounds. Under my feet thin grass crept up through the crusty soils. Halfway across the vast field I was accosted by the first wave of boatmen, the vanguard of Allahabad's spiritual businessmen. These are the men who row the boats that ferry pilgrims out to where the three rivers converge.

The crowd grew as I moved closer to the water, and I tried to ignore their persistent wailing, "BO-AT, BO-AT, COME, COME." It was an "in your face" hard sell. I knew that I needed a pilot to get me out into the stream but I didn't want to succumb to this overzealous pleading for my money. But as I approached the beach I saw an old man quietly tying up his boat for the night.

He stood up when he saw my interest, put his hands on his hips, smiled and said, "Welcome for cheap price." We agreed on ten rupees. The boat was surrounded by the young vultures who had tracked me. They all grimaced as I made the deal, and all shouted at once, "I give you better price." My ancient pilot pushed off, glanced back at his younger competition and cackled sarcastically to them, "Bye, bye."

Shankar Lall, my navigator, was a veteran of the boat trade. He wore the white dhoti of a brahmin, under which was a body thinner than that of the cranes that populated the river's shallow waters. He sported a pair of red-rimmed glasses in the style of third world bureaucrats and his mouth was toothless except for three crumpled fangs that emerged endearingly when he smiled.

Time had mellowed him. He enjoyed rowing and sang droning devotional songs as he pulled us through the water. It was a pleasure to watch him on the oars, for he was the master of his craft. His bamboo blades sliced the river smoothly and through those long appendages he felt her currents.

There was a methodical creak, creak from the right oar lock with each dip. It was the mantra of hard work. The creak meshed with the call of the seagulls swooping overhead, marine birds hundreds of kilometers from the ocean. I liked those sounds — they were echos from my childhood, early mornings on the water, in my leaky rowboat, pulling on the oars and thinking.

Eventually Shankar decided to try out his English on me. "You call me Chacha-ji. Means uncle . . . OK?"

Then he tried an explanation of the three rivers. "Tirveni, three rivers. You know?" He laughed, "Yamuna, green water. Ganga-mai, white water. Saraswati, milk water . . . You know?" Then he laughed again. "I like milk . . . But I don't see Saraswati."

Off to our right two boatloads of shaven-headed male devotees passed by. Their boatmen strained under a load a dozen times heavier than Chacha-ji's, so it was no wonder he was laughing. The passengers all chanted loud, marine corps style mantras, "JAI GANGA, HAI. . . . JAI JAMUNA, HAI . . . JAI, SARASWATI, HAI . . . " It was a river-

58

borne cult initiation, skin-head Hindus, all shouting to be heard by the Gods. But they were a non-aggressive sect, and they waved at us frantically, a joy-ridden group of fraternity brothers.

Shankar was rowing against time. Ahead the sun was falling and we needed to reach the sangam before dark. We arrived just as the ruby disk touched the far horizon.

A sandbar separated the two flows a few hundred meters out into the confluence. Along it was moored a flotilla of boats and floating temples. At these temporary docking points all along this makeshift puja ground a frenzy of religious business was taking place. Hundreds of people had gathered around this riverine shrine. Prayers were being shouted, clouds of incense did battle overhead, and the air was alive with flower offerings being tossed to the gods.

Into this religious maelstrom Shankar rowed. A squabble had erupted at the berth to our right and one of the antagonists leapt onto our vessel. It was a pirate boarding.

He approached me smiling, with beetle juice stained teeth, a severed coconut in one hand and a wilted garland of flowers in the other. He glowered at me and in heavily accented English offered "a most auspicious puja in honor of the three goddesses. Prayers that will, most definitely, guarantee long life, wealth, plentiful children, and a beautiful bride all . . . for one low price." I declined his offer and he immediately lowered the cost. I had no desire to have this man spoil the atmosphere of the sangam and so declined again and asked Shankar to pull away. The pujari made a disgruntled leap back to his home turf and scowled at us as we recaught the river current.

Chacha-ji laughed. The light was gone; the rivers had met in silence beneath us. I had felt nothing overwhelming but had sensed something peaceful even amidst the raucous religious transactions. We had accomplished our goal.

Shankar pulled on the oars and the boat creaked slowly back upstream and eventually into the sandy shore. We landed quietly with a sandy hiss and Chacha-ji jumped off nimbly with the bowline.

I paid Shankar his ten rupees plus ten rupees more. The goddess had loosened my wallet, but Chacha-ji looked at me incredulously and said, "Little brother, that was a fifty rupee row." I laughed, slapped him on the back and said, "Maybe next time." He grinned, a twinkle in his eye and said, "Maybe next time you will bring your own Goddess!"

Back across the mela ground the sun had set and the sky was dark. I moved through puff dust and loose sand, and looking back over my shoulder I could see a three-quarter moon hanging over the sangam.

The next morning I was up before dawn and heading down to the Yamuna. I made my way along a trail following the northern bank. The river was silent in the half light but as the sun rose an audible soundscape accompanied it: the splash of early morning bathers, the thump of clothes being smashed into cleanliness, the chatter of fishermen, the hollering of boatmen. India is a panorama of noise. Noise is vibration, and to a Hindu vibration is life. For Indians it is important to be surrounded by the din of existence.

I walked past the sheer, sandstone walls of Jhunsi fort. The castle is built on the high ground between the converging rivers. The flows merge in a feminine triangle of land, the Ganga and Yamuna, the two thighs, the invisible Saraswati the molten vagina. In the anthropomorphic symbology of Hinduism the fort has been built on mother earth's clitoris! Chance? I thought not, for what better way to stimulate armies.

Past the garrison I crossed back onto the mela ground. The sand stretched on and on, the Ganga off in the invisible future. In the distance I could hear the drums and horns of some medieval carnival and soon a procession of Hindus marched by, led by drummers in rags and slow-paced, spotless Brahmins.

A rogue breeze picked up and the dust rose in sporadic bursts. I put my right hand over my forehead to shade my eyes and out of the shadows walked a single man.

He was a naked saddhu — his skin, dark from the relentless sun was iced in a coating of powdered earth. His face was deeply lined, but without emotion. His rat-tailed dreadlocks swung to and fro in time with his gait. His penis lay exposed, resting in thick nest of dusty pubic hair. The saddhu walked with precision, measuring his steps silently. We drew abreast. I smiled, then he smiled. His teeth were the color of blood and his mouth's moistness caught the sun and glistened. He bowed his head and moved on.

I topped a small hillock and saw the meeting point. Out in midstream a fleet of pilgrim boats crowded the pujari docks, platforms for the faithful. As I moved closer I could hear the shouts of children, the holy call of conch shells, the braying of a lonesome dog. I entered the drama of the sangam tentatively, like a child, excited and nervous about a trip to the circus. The sangam was a full blossoming of the theater of Hinduism. Around me business, pleasure and the challenges of higher realization were woven as seamlessly as the rivers.

Lolling pujaris lay on wooden benches awaiting their next customers, shifty-eyed trinket salesmen sat in multicolored booths, saddhus meditated cross-legged and undisturbed, pilgrims huddled in tight circles discussing loudly the next step in their religious holidays, and through it all children screamed, running figure eights around tea stalls and bangle shops.

By the water's edge I stopped again. Behind me the circus raged on. Before me in the hazy afternoon light I watched two naked boys sprint across the river shallows. The water splashed up, transformed into diamonds, and showers of jewels haloed them. They were dancing on the line between worlds.

Vindyachal lies half way between Allahabad and Varanasi in eastern Uttar Pradesh. It is a region known for feudal landlords and private armies. It is the kind of place where news clips regularly report that entire trains have been boarded and looted. The kind of place where the police advise people to bar their windows and secure their doors after dark. But this is not a recent phenomenon. Vindyachal is the historic base for the legendary fraternity of Indian highwaymen, the Thuggis.

The organization may be dead, but their legend lives on. The temple around which the town is built pays homage to Kali, the goddess of death who was the patron deity of the Thuggis. She is the dark and powerful antithesis of Ganga's compassionate energy. On festival days tens of thousands of pilgrims crush themselves into the queues surrounding the temple just to glimpse the image held in the inner sanctum, the same statue that imbued the Thuggis with their legendary strength. The Thuggis may be part of history but Kali and her phenomenal power are timeless.

Vindyachal is a classic example of the Indian temple town. Religious cities like Allahabad and Varanasi have large enough populations that they can foster indigenous industries. Vindyachal, on the other hand, exists solely because of its temple. The town is a tribute to Kali, but at the same time it connects her with her twin sister, Ganga. Vindhyachal is a transition point, a bridge between the two facets of the mother goddess.

The town itself is a spiral to the center. The outer edges, the spiral's entry, are the faintly buzzing residential areas. The shops and stalls that surround the main complex are the first step inwards. They rattled with the business of religion, salesmen hustling for their daily bread.

Farther in was the cordoned off lineup of devotees encircling the temple, shuffling slowly to the inner sanctum. With them was an air of frenzied feelings, shouts and yelling, accusations and counter-accusations. It was a flurry of emotion before the storm.

The entrance to the inner sanctum was jammed with distorted bodies. The screams of the faithful being ravished by the power of the goddess's darshan inside reverberated and amplified out the marble doorway. The image of the goddess was the center, the threshold between Vindyachal and another state of mind.

But the other face of the Mother lay just four hundred meters to the south, just outside the town's inward spiral. There, down a steep flight of stairs, flanked on both sides by an endless stretch of sand, was the Ganga. At Vindhyachal the river flows by without fanfare; she is as silent as her alter ego is voluble. Here too the pujaris sat, waiting quietly, rather than jostling for their clients. Here also flower garlands were for sale, proffered by scrawny cherubs in rags, tiny salespeople whose effervescent smiles forced coins from unwilling pockets.

Here, beyond the shouting and brush of bodies, was the peace where contemplation could stir and crazy logic could work its way towards the truth. The river flows on timelessly, evoking a compassion that forces her worshippers' quiet desires to be exposed.

Ganga-mai is the silent mirror. Kali is fear stripped raw.

Kashi, "the city of light" — this is how Varanasi, the city between the Varana and the Asi rivers, is known to Hindus. There, for the first of only three times, the Ganga makes a wide sweep to the north. South is the direction of ignorance and death, north is the way to wisdom and life.

It is at Varanasi that the earthly Ganga most closely resembles her celestial self. Of all the places where she is revered and propitiated it is at Kashi where she is most powerful.

But Kashi is also the city of Shiva and it is Shiva who "tamed" Ganga-mai. It was Shiva who tempted her to earth and who absorbed, in his mighty dreadlocks, her angry fall to this reality. He was the one who rid her of her idle pride and facilitated for the tempestuous goddess another level of wisdom, and it is Shiva who eventually made her his wife.

Ganga and Shiva are inextricably linked in Kashi and it is here, in the presence of his tempering wife, that the Hindu lord of life and death is most approachable.

As the ancient Kashi Khanda text states, "The Ganges, Shiva and Kashi. Where this trinity is watchful no wonder here is found the grace that leads one on to perfect bliss."

Varanasi is a city of extremes. Good and evil, life and death, it is the truest dwelling of the chaos that has created India.

To discover more about the enigma of Varanasi I met with Dr. Rana Singh, a professor in geography and an expert on sacred landscape.

Dr. Singh was a "healthy" looking man, a term that in India means he had a fair sized belly and a good head of hair. He was a man of stories, quick bursts of humor and twinkling eyes. It was obvious that he was an engaging lecturer. Rana-ji's tales started off slow but soon his delight in the narrative would overtake him and by the end he was dancing with his own words.

He explained that the most difficult part to comprehend about Varanasi is that trapped between its three defining rivers it is a microcosm of all India. Within the city's sacred triangle everything that is good and bad, and the extremes of each, is played out. The city was most suited for those on the arduous path to higher realization, those who had come to terms with the fact that the angelic and the evil are just different sides of the same coin.

Rana-ji said, "A folk saying in Benares has it that until you are beaten and humiliated, you have not experienced Kashi." He went on to tell me and my friend Kaja how he, a university professor, in protecting a French academic colleague, had been mugged by a gang of thugs who included some of his own students.

He told the story with a smile. It was a rite of passage, something he had accepted in order to reside in the city he loved. The doctor lived with the knowledge that dwelling in the city of the gods would not always be heaven.

The entity that defines Varanasi is the river. The city would not exist without the Ganga, for it is the definitive feature of Kashi. Ganga-mai is the purity that enables the "city of light" to be the earthly abode of the Hindu world's celestial beings. But the river, Varanasi's fluid spinal cord, is yet another of the Kashi's many dichotomies.

Early one morning while exploring the west bank underneath the railway bridge that marks the city's northern limit, I found myself slipping on a greasy, stinking mass of fresh human waste. Looking around in the shade of the bridge's pillars I saw dozens of men squatting, their pants down around their ankles, grunting with the satisfaction of intestinal release.

I can only attribute this confusing use of the mother's flow for a public washroom as a result of the people's belief in the goddess's incorruptibility (and a distinct lack of municipal infrastructure). What difference, the man blissfully evacuating himself must ask, will one person's waste make to the great, stainless being of the mother?

Unfortunately when the 300 million Indians of the Gangeatic Plains all line up and defecate in Hinduism's circulatory system it does make a difference. The Swatcha Ganga movement (Clean Ganga movement) has reported that upstream from the city coliform counts are thirteen times the safe limit, while downstream the level has reached 300 times the allowable limit.

In the early 1990s the Indian government under Rajiv Ghandi promised hundreds of millions of rupees to be spent on cleaning up the river. The plan called for an overall improvement of organic waste disposal, limits on the amount of discharged industrial effluent, and the establishment of a chain of electric crematoriums. The desire to have your final rites performed by the Ganga is almost universal in Hinduism. Advances on all these fronts have been negligible, and the government's campaign has been a complete failure.

The project is probably best characterized by one of its more novel schemes, the introduction into the river of 28,000 flesh eating turtles. The hope was that they would rid the Varanasi area of the dangerously decomposing half-cremated corpses that litter the shore downstream from the city. For a while it appeared to be working, but then the village people discovered that turtle flesh tasted similar to chicken and a new local delicacy was created, turtle curry. Now not a single turtle is to be found in the river.

V.B. Mishra is the man most responsible for the increased awareness of the river's dilemma. He is the head of the Swatcha Ganga group, a professor of hydrology at Benares Hindu University and the head, or Mahant, of the Sankat Mochan Mandir, one of the five most popular temples in the city. He is eminently qualified to discuss the scientific and spiritual concerns of the Ganga.

I met him on a cold January evening at his group's headquarters in the southern part of the city. He shuffled into the room and filled the air with old age. His hair was the same color as his undyed woolen shawl and his face was deeply lined with a tiredness that had seeped into his soul. He looked like a broken monarch, a king in need of sleep. His lack of energy was evidence of just how much he had invested in the problems of his beloved Ganga.

I asked him what he thought about the folk beliefs concerning the river's perpetual purity and ability to clean herself. He immediately let out an exasperated groan and asked if I thought that self-regulating organisms have a limit to how much they can absorb. His point was that, yes, the river can clean itself, but only to a certain point. The Ganga had reached the point of saturation and we were now consciously killing her.

The atmosphere in the room was morose. Sweets and tea were served in silence and a gray cloud hung over the room. We chatted more, but it was clear that he wasn't in the mood.

V.B. Mishra was being beaten by Mother India's massive, inertia driven bureaucracy, her inefficient, uncompassionate alter-ego. The millions that had been allocated to catalyze a new pragmatic attitude towards the river had been squandered in the offices of faceless civil servants. He had the most worthy cause in the world, but the powers that be were not willing to follow through on their promises. He was being worked over by the minions of mediocrity. The Ganga was dying a slow, painful death in the dark, dusty, ledger filled offices of the Indian government.

Possibly the most obvious example of Rana Singh's dichotomous Kashi is the business of dying. Varanasi is the "Great Tirtha," the cosmic ford, the most auspicious place to cross from this world to the next. People come from all over India to spend their last weeks or years in Kashi. It is there on the most propitious northern sweep of the Ganga that Hindus want their last rites to be performed. With a monopoly on the geography of death Varanasi has created its own commercial caste of deathly businessmen.

The city is congested with old folks homes, hospices, clinics and private hospitals, but it is at the burning ghats, the open air, wood-fired crematoriums that death and money most intertwine.

Manikarnika Ghat is the greatest of these. Here freshly deceased bodies are brought, wrapped in silks and trimmed in gold, shouldered by shouting processions of bearers. There, after lengthy prayers and chanting, the remains are cremated in an aromatic bonfire of sandalwood. The ashes are retrieved and sprinkled on the Ganga, purification by fire and water performed within the precincts of the city of Shiva. With these complete the way is clear for the journey onwards.

Manikarnika is a Brueghelian image of the charnel ground — figures move in every direction with purpose, and massive stone buildings look down on the hissing body fires. Tight into the beach are the freighter boats carrying the cremation wood, gigantic dories loaded to the waterline with chunky slabs of timber. The perpetual fires leave a distorted haze over the area, a grayish sweat that dulls the edges of the scene. The vista from above is a sepia-toned composition, the sand, the wood, the stone of the surrounding palaces, the boats, bow first into the shore, the shirtless firemen, darkened by the sun, the beige-robed pujaris, grave as they chant the final rites, eyes closed.

Into this earth tone landscape come the bodies, visual feasts for color starved eyes, lumpen masses wrapped in the brightest scarlets and yellows, sparkling with gold tinsel, draped in the saffron of Hinduism.

All these colors will be eaten by the fire. All that will be left will be a naked corpse writhing in the heat of the enclosing flames. The skin will wriggle as if still alive, the face will melt from the smooth skull, the fingertips will tremble in anticipation. The skull will explode with a sharp pop and the muscle and bone shall become more fuel for the final fire.

At Manikarnika the body as we know it disappears. The ashes are all that is left of the vessel that we cherish, and those are gathered by the family and priest and immersed in the river, the only timeless body in Hinduism.

I crossed the border between Uttar Pradesh and Bihar through a herd of cattle that numbered in the thousands. On the north side of the river a guy-mela, a cattle fair, was underway. Subcontinental cowboys from all over the region had traveled there to sell their stock, but any idea of similarities between this and a prairie livestock auction were quickly subdued. The haggling went on in small circles under tropical trees and makeshift canvas tarps. The bargainers huddled in mumbling groups, looking more like biblical shepherds than range riders.

The cattle were, for the most part, ghostly, skeletal apparitions, draft animals on their last legs. It was a market of bones and flesh for the highest bidder, a venue for the relocation of skinny animals to skinny men.

Out of the guy-mela and across the Ganga I rolled into Bihar on a concrete and steel bridge that appeared centuries ahead of the cattle fair. Bihar is India's wild west, the state that bottoms lists on almost every category of modernity. Bihar, as an Indian friend once told me, is "Ruled by gangsters, administered by the corrupt and policed by the immoral. Watch yourself there, Jono."

Buxar, the settlement on the south side of the bridge, appeared to live up to the state's reputation. It was dusty and hot and none of disintegrating buildings, except the century old railway station, seemed to have been built with the future in mind. It had noisy pretensions, as trucks and tractors blared along the partly paved streets and cyclists and rickshaw-wallahs rang their bells at every opportunity. But Buxar was really nothing more than a large village.

Down by the river activity was high as a few dozen men were busy bashing together bamboo platforms that would accommodate pilgrims coming to celebrate Buxar's role in the Ramayana. It was here that Ram and his brother Laksman, while guarding the temple of their guru Viswanamitra, had slain a group of demons related to their archenemy, Ravana. The deaths sowed the seeds for the epic's main act.

I went in search of the principal temple only to find it closed and barred. I sat in the courtyard, a little depressed, and quickly gathered a crowd of ogling, inquisitive kids. I was wishing for their disappearance when one of them squealed in excitement, "The baba wants to speak." Simultaneously the dreadlocked head of a saddhu appeared two stories above us over the top of the temple's roof wall.

He was coated in ash and on his forehead were painted the three upward strokes of the followers of Vishnu. The children were squirming in anticipation. The baba spoke in deep toned, Oxford accented, theater English. "Welcome, foreigner, to the site of Rama's battle, his glorious first encounter with the family of evil incarnate. Such an encounter could only happen on the banks of the super mega holy Ganga life stream . . . "

The saddhu's thirty minute account of Buxar's place in the religious geography of Hindustan dragged on like a bad radio play. At the end of it all he stood, very proud of himself, with his hands on his dusty, naked hips, gazing out over the river, his focus on nothing in particular.

I was in shock. Had I stumbled on some wandering performance artist or was this multilingual saddhu on a quest that I just couldn't fathom? The children, still rapt with attention, were wide-eyed in awe.

The baba looked down on us with a gaze that conveyed a feeling of "I am holier than thou" and then said, "Please leave your donation in the box below." With that he disappeared again behind the roof wall.

I stopped at the entrance and found a tin box, painted red, with SUPERMEGAHOLYGANGA BABA stenciled in white on it. I dropped two rupees into it, in appreciation of the entertainment factor.

Patna is the capital of Bihar, a city whose history is a roll call for India's bygone glories. Patilaputra, as it was known in its heyday, is built on a high bank on the south side of the Ganga, and when the river is in monsoon flood the city can become an island on a watery plain. Its strategic position controlling the river and the Sone valley routes to the south made it the logical capital for a string of successive empires from as far back as 500 BCE.

It was the seat of the great Buddhist Emperor Ashoka, the birthplace of Guru Nanak, the founder of the Sikh religion, and the site of formative teachings by the Buddha, the Jain masters and a string of Hindu pandits. But these days Patna is a city in decay, a center held together by a bare semblance of administration and the most minimal infrastructure.

Maybe it is because of this chaos that Patna seems to exude a certain style. Patna is confused and distant but there is something subliminally intriguing about the city. Among the ruins of Mughal and British empires and between the crumbling icons of the modern India there are a swag of architectural diamonds. They are buildings that have been maintained by individual families for centuries, elegant, pillared houses with open verandahs and beautifully worked details, and homes whose stonework has been worn smooth with the generations and whose thresholds speak of personal histories. Patna is quaint: like a mildly senile grandmother, wearing a turban and speaking without ego about her past adventures. It is a far away and exotic place.

I spent my first morning there being shuffled between government offices trying to unearth information on the city. The bureaucrats could tell the times and frequency of flights and trains to Calcutta and Delhi, but were of no use in shedding light on the Patna's history. They were experts in leaving the city but had no interest in its roots.

I went back to my hotel on the main road where I decided that Patna was probably the noisiest city in India. Looking down from my fourth story balcony I could see that the traffic flowed with no pattern. The idea of two orderly lanes was lost in the clamor. Below me was a mechanized version of the venous system, thousands of red and white blood cells moving forward in a jerky, pinballing motion. The bumper car procession was accompanied by the discordant blare of transport truck air horns, the screech of motorbikes, the gurgling snarl of motorscooters, the frenetic tinkling of rickshaw bells and the bloodcurdling howls of drivers in the throes of road rage.

To escape the decibel nightmare I went in search of the river. I found her through a maze of alleys and lanes stacked with people and livestock.

In one passage, trapped between a pair of multistoried banks, I discovered a community that looked as if it had been transplanted as a set piece from the countryside to the city. Smooth-walled mud huts, with gracefully curving lines and folk frescoes adorning their doorways, sat in a lane populated with chai drinking bankers, hurried looking brokers and the ubiquitous cows.

At the river I was once again shocked by the peace that she brought to the surroundings. But in Patna it felt different. Maybe it was the influence of the city's unadorned style but, while her quietude remained, the deep stillness was gone. The river felt vulnerable.

The point gelled for me when I stopped at a nearby riverside shrine and had a chat with the resident baba. I told him of my feelings and he nodded. "Yes, well this may have some truth. The entire way from her source Ganga-mai is purifying all in her midst. The evidence for this is seen in her clear, clean waters in the beginnings. Now we see that she is dirty and slow. She has been absorbing the dirt of India for over 1,500 kilometers. She is tired."

I decided to walk east along the riverbank to what is billed as the longest river bridge in the world, the seven kilometer span that links Patna to the Ganga's north shore. The bank was steep and muddy and surprisingly devoid of people. The odd launderer and the Victorian-fronted Patna Swimming Club were the only human interludes.

For the length of its passage through the city I saw no religious ghats and no one taking a cleansing dip. It was sad to see the river, the focus around which the city had been founded, relegated to the background.

It was in Patna that I began to see the Ganga as a commercial entity. For the first time I saw large boats moving on the river. Steel barges and wide-beamed dhows from Calcutta and Diamond Harbor, rusty scows pushed by chugging diesels and iron wood relics with tattered sails made their way east and west.

I was fascinated by the sailboats, a physical connection between the millennia. Downriver the dhows would set their sails full to assist the current's pull. But upriver on calm days they were towed by their crews, teams of five or six men all tied into a main line attached to the ship's mast. They were human draft animals. It was a task that, dependent on the winds, could continue for hundreds of kilometers. It was an archaic job, men tethered to a sailing ship weighted down with building stone or sand, walking in the shadows of twenty-story office blocks.

The commerce of the river moved at a completely different pace than that of the city. There was a cadence to the loading and unloading of the ships that suited the river's flow. The men moved in a pensive methodical way that spoke of their acceptance of the way things were. They were busy enough to not be bothered by my presence, but not so rushed that they couldn't chat amongst themselves.

The scene at the bridge was yet another of India's constant juxtapositions. Before me stood a concrete span so long its end was lost in the midday haze. It was a modernist masterpiece of symmetrical sequence, squares and triangles fighting against the organic patterning of the river. Yet the area around it was a barrio of rough hovels, lean-tos and shelters of the most temporary kind. The air was thick with the dung smoke of cooking fires and the smell of fresh excrement. Around me the whoosh of the river wind moving through the mighty arches was mixed with the constant call of babies and the tinny sound of radio music. The bridge was the cathedral in whose shadow those people lived.

I headed back to my hotel room and after battling the stampede of Patna traffic arrived exhausted, only to find my bed covered in a scattering of rat shit. I called the floor attendant who looked at me incredulously and said, "Sir, I believe you left your bathroom door open?" The door was definitely open. He looked at me in a humorously questioning way. "Well sir, this rat is always coming in through the bathroom door."

Without cleaning up, the old man departed, leaving me to believe that this particular rat was common knowledge among travelers to Bihar.

On the train to Monghyr I had the good fortune to meet with Raj Chatterjee, a 20-something-year-old man with a mod hair cut and expensive prescription glasses. I was impressed by his ability to read an Indian rock and roll magazine in the jostling of the train's general ticket compartment and to wear a nylon ski jacket in 28°Celsius weather.

At first I was a little suspicious of him as his dress and demeanor removed him a century or so from our dhoti-clad compartment colleagues. But slowly he drew me into a conversation on the woes of his beloved India and it evolved that his interests ranged far and wide. Raj was a Bengali from Patna whose posting as a sales rep for a large cement company had brought him, as a bachelor, to what he called "the backwater of Monghyr."

As the train pulled into the station, dusk was falling and Raj quickly hustled me off the platform, saying, "This is not a good place to be after dark." We boarded a shared taxi already overflowing with passengers and headed downtown. There Raj arranged a room in the town's only hotel and took me out to dinner.

At the clapboard restaurant where he and Monghyr's other displaced bachelors regularly ate we had a sumptuous feast of curried eggplant and tandoori roti. The atmosphere was one of homely male bonding, with lots of laughing and talk of far away families. We stayed until closing, sipping tea under crackling fluorescent lights while I was gently interrogated about places my new friends had only dreamed of. When the restaurant's stately owner finally nudged us out the door Raj and Amresh, his best friend, announced that they would escort me the next morning on a "whirlwind tour of Monghyr." As they said, "Jono, we really want to freak out with you." I wasn't sure whether to be worried or excited.

My guides arrived the next morning at 7 a.m., knocking hard on my hotel door and announcing with a flourish that I should "throw off the blankets and embrace this most beautiful day." With huge smiles the pair admitted that they had been up until dawn, chatting about "everything and anything." I began to see that Raj's nickname, Chatty, was more than just a shortening of his surname.

We headed out into the misty chill of the Bihari morning. The three of us jammed onto the bench seat of a wobbly pedal rickshaw piloted by a ragged ancient in dire need of a bath. I sat imperiously in the middle while Raj and Amresh let their legs dangle over each side.

At the river we stopped at a sandstone shrine that looked to the west. In the last few hundred kilometers the river had grown massive. It spread itself across the landscape, defying ideas of banks and borders, and as the morning fog began to rise it was difficult to distinguish between land and water, the two worlds becoming one.

Raj and Amresh explained, rapidly and dramatically, that Monghyr too had a part to play in the Ramayana. It was here, on the banks of the river, that Sita had rid herself of the doubts surrounding her kidnapping by the demon Ravana. Lord Ram, her husband, had questioned his wife's purity during imprisonment and so to cure him of all suspicions she had thrown herself to Agni, the god of fire. To prove her virtue to the doubting Ram, Sita took her own life.

It is a mythological act that has repercussions to this day. Despite legislation and attempts at modernization, Indian wives, to show their undying devotion, still occasionally committ "sutti" and throw themselves on their husband's funeral pyres.

From the river we moved inland to a site where historically the Ganga had flowed. There, at the temple of Chandnitan inside a small hot cave, is the eye of Parvati.

Legend has it that Parvati, Shiva's first wife, was extremely jealous of the relationship between Shiva and Ganga, and at the culmination of one of their not infrequent arguments Parvati became so incensed that she literally exploded. Her body parts rose to the heavens and rained down all across the subcontinent. Now, wherever these "landing sites" have been recognized, they are revered as earthly emanations of the goddess and temples have been raised in her honor.

Chandnitan is a hot, damp, dark cave, claustrophobic when holding only four people and unimaginable with more. It is believed that here the eye of the goddess came to earth. On an altar against the rear wall of the grotto sits a gold and silver sculpture shaped something like an upturned nut dish. Behind this lies Parvati's eye, the proverbial vision of the gods. The thought is intoxicating, but the scenario's catch-22 is that anyone who attempts to take away the metallic cover is immediately blinded.

Raj was visibly struck by the legends and asked the pujari to perform a special ritual for him. The thin priest relished the tale and in recounting the legend he dwelt on the many morbid stories told about horrific loss of sight. Peculiarly his own eyes seemed incapable of focusing. They moved in out-of-sync patterns as he salivatingly recounted the sight-stealing powers of his shrine. Whether his eye problems were the influence of the goddess or the effect of the hallucinogenic datura plants that adorned the altar I couldn't be sure.

He completed the prayer ceremony quickly. Raj was happy but then the pujari asked for an outrageous fee and an argument ensued. Accusations raged back and forth with Amresh and myself eventually dragging Raj out of the temple. I was shocked that Raj had eventually paid the asked for amount, but my friend impatiently explained, "Of course I had to. If I didn't the puja would not have been effective. The prayers are worth more than money. The ugliness of that pujari was in his inability to barter."

Nerves settled as we made our way back to the river and by the time we had returned to the riverside shrine Raj was back to his talkative self. We sat on the ghat and watched fishermen toss their nets out into the still water. The far bank was still unseen, the morning mist replaced by a midday haze. From the temple the priest recited rhyming passages from the Ramayana. It felt comfortable.

Soon I would leave and Raj, in that fraternal way that makes some western men nervous, took my hand. He told me that when he missed me he would come to the river, listen to the Doors on his Walkman, and watch the Ganga make her quiet way past.

I was a little taken aback by his emotion but was touched by his friendship and how he could find comfort in the river. Maybe there was a new set of values, and a different set of mantras, but it was grounding to know that a new generation still felt an attachment to the river. I told Raj that I thought Jim Morrison would approve.

From Monghyr I moved on to Sultanganj. It is there that the Ganga makes its second auspicious turn to the north, and to honor her movement the magnificent Ajgaivi temple has been built. I searched for the shrine for hours, surprised at my difficulty in finding it. It is often pictured in guidebooks as a dramatic island cloister perched atop a cluster of gargantuan boulders and encircled by the swirling river. But I could find nothing like it along the river banks, and it was only after retracing my steps for a third time that I finally realized how it had been there all along.

Just east of the town a rocky knoll topped with a white temple was surrounded by shocking yellow fields of mustard flowers. It was landlocked but familiar, for though the winter river had shrunk and lay seven hundred meters to the north, in monsoon flood this same hillock would be entrapped by the swollen river. The Ajgaivi temple's identity was as seasonal as the river's.

Tracked by half a dozen villagers I circumambulated the island. I admired the handsome rock carvings around its base and marveled at the solidity of the architecture in an ever changing landscape.

It was a brilliant day, cool but bright, and after half an hour of watching my every move the curious audience abruptly announced that they would make me tea. From the pack of one a kerosene stove was produced, from the satchel of another fresh milk, and from the bag of a third a paper packet of loose tea. After noisy and ritualistic preparations we all sat as a half circle in the sand and with the brush of the river breeze, the background chug of the stove and cups of sweet chai in hand, our little band silently admired the Ganga's gracious sweep to the north.

It is because of this anomalous turn in the river that Sultanganj is designated the starting point for the annual Dev Ghar pilgrimage.

The journey is an arduous act of devotion that requires the participants to walk with a vial of pure Ganga water 300 kilometers south to the Shiva temple of Dev Ghar. There the lingam in the main shrine is said to get so heated from its potential energy that only the liquid of the goddess can cool it down.

The event is a national occurrence — in 1998 700,000 Hindus were involved. It is an act that draws people from every age and walk of life. Businessmen walk beside peasants, grandparents stroll hand in hand with grandchildren, and the infirm shuffle along next to the Dak Bhums, the men and women who run the route, bringing themselves to ecstasy by pushing the limits of their physical capabilities.

The pilgrimage is usually undertaken during the summer rainy season but on the town's main street I came upon a pair of old men who were just beginning the trip south. They were committed ascetics who would prostrate and pray with each step. It was a painstakingly slow process that intensified their devotion and extended the length of their pilgrimage from days to months.

They were ancient souls. Their skin, stretched tight over their bony frames, was the color of autumn leaves. Their hair, in knotted dreads, hung low on their backs. Their only coverings were rough cotton loincloths. They were the simplest of pilgrims. They had dismissed the formalities of appearance; for them the body was a medium, not an image to glorify.

They moved in unison, one just slightly ahead of the other. They stood, palms together at their foreheads, then dropped onto their knees stretching out to full length, arms directly forward as if diving across the dusty pavement. Then from this arrow straight extension they would raise themselves, the mantra of Shiva on their breath, and start the motion again from the point marked by the farthest extent of their fingers.

They were a clockwork image of devotion that nothing — the traffic, the pedestrians, the ponderous cows, or the filth on the street — could interfere with. Their mission was ahead and everything else was superfluous.

From the thriving pilgrimage site at Sultanapur I moved back a thousand years to Vikramashila. Vikramashila was, a millennium ago, one of a trio of great Buddhist universities that had flourished in Bihar's golden age. Their reputation was known around the world with students traveling to study from as far away as Iran, Indonesia and China. In its day Vikramashila had been at the center of world thought.

To get there I had rented a pony cart at the railway station in Batthar. It was a jaunty two-wheeled affair with a red tasseled yellow canopy and seats covered in blue vinyl. The driver was a cheerful character with a tight belly hidden beneath his sparkling dhoti and a handlebar mustache to die for. I had initially chosen the cart because his horse seemed the healthiest of a scrawny genre but was pleased that the driver was as jovial as his gelding was energetic.

The way led through lush countryside following along the Ganga. Vikramashila had been built close to the river, but over the centuries the river had slid north and now the surrounding area was a vision of plains India. Rice paddies assembled in a Mondrian geometry were bordered by thick jungle that, in our passing, sprung to life with the call of a dozen species of tropical birds. The village people working the fields were indifferently busy, moving steadily at that half speed pace that defines Third World agriculture.

We arrived at the hottest time of the day. The area around the ruins was deserted and anyone associated with them had fled for the shade. I was alone in the presence of an architectural enigma. To the neighboring peasants it was an obstruction in their daily lives, a mound of bricks that made their lives busier than need be. Yet to India it was an integral piece of a glorious past, a space that whispered of a thousand debates and a million calls to the pen.

The ruins had appeared out of nowhere, the site a strange assemblage of partly excavated knolls and depressions. From a distance it could have been the remains of some disused brickworks, but as we got closer I saw a symmetry that belied deep architectural thought. Foundations and remaining walls radiated out from a central structure, a Buddhist stupa. The stupa is an architectural representation of everything that the Buddha implies and the focus around which Vikramashila functions.

Girdling the base of it I discovered terracotta friezes set with Buddhist symbols: the twelve auspicious signs, the pantheon of the gods, Buddhas displaying different hand gestures or mudras. All were worn to the point of indiscernability, but all retained some form of faded voice. One in particular held my imagination. It was of a meditating Buddha, legs crossed in lotus position, hands laid gently across his thighs, head firm but relaxed, perfectly set on his squared shoulders. There was so much to read in that square foot of primordial clay. Yet the relief figure had completely disappeared, and all that remained was a shadow of the original three-dimensional image. The tile was a microcosm of Vikramashila, a shadow that sparked memory and imagination.

On Bihar's western border, just inside Bengal, it is impossible to ignore the Farraka Barrage. Vikramashila is the ancient India, Farraka is the modern. The barrage is a flow control dam that stretches the entire width of the river only kilometers from the Bangladeshi border. It operates to control the huge seasonal fluctuations of the Ganga and more importantly to increase the flow of water into the Hooghly, the river of Calcutta. Without this extra water the Hooghly would silt up and marine traffic to the third largest city in the world would halt.

But the Farraka barrage is also the trademark of India's riverine nationalism. International treaties concerning the flow of the Ganga are under constant debate, and thus the dam works for the benefit of India and the detriment of Bangladesh. It gives India the power to control the flow of water that enters its neighbor, and since Bangladesh possesses the most water per capita of any country in the world, this means that India controls its life.

The fact is reinforced as you approach the barrage. Signs proclaiming "PROTECTED PLACE" and "NO PHOTOGRAPHY ALLOWED" glare at you from rusty girders and barbed wire fences. It looks more like a military installation than a civil engineering project.

As I approached the guard post that marks the entrance to the structure the soldiers inside snapped to attention. One strode out onto the road that crowns the dam and stopped in front of me with his hand outstretched in a gesture of need. It was an unspoken passport check. I gave him my papers, which he proceeded to scrutinize upside down, for English was not his first language. He returned them with a stern face and ushered me into his empire.

I walked out only a hundred meters onto the dam, merely wanting to see the bifurcation of the rivers and the effect that such an obstruction would produce in the goddess. The flow was thick and stagnated, a brackish pond that stretched off into the unseeable distance. The blurred sun reflected on its surface, a bleached stain on the fabric of the river. It was a depressing place. The positivism that I associated with the river had been eaten here by its wholesale conscription by a single country, a single religion and a single mythology. Narrow-minded reason and nationalism controlled the barrage, and my only consolation was the hope that, like Maneri and Tehri, Farraka would be a temporary blemish on the Ganga's fluid continuum.

I got lost trying to find Hurare Duare, an out of place Italinate palace in the middle of Bengal. I found myself wandering along a dirt path through a series of mud brick villages. Eventually a shoeless schoolboy silently took me by the hand and led me back to the road. I hadn't said a word, but as the twelve-year-old hailed down a pedal rickshaw and ushered me on board he said in English, "White people don't come to our village. I think you want to go to Hurare Duare."

In repayment for the local ruler's help in their campaign against the French the British built the palace in 1757. The Murshid Quli Khan rose to power in the early part of the eighteenth century. He constructed his capital, Murshidabad, on the Bengali tributary of the Ganga, and used his position to create one of India's first centralized administrations. Murshid Khan was so competent in fact that his buzzing little kingdom became the prototype for the subcontinent's next two centuries of European imperialism.

Murshidabad had its time in the sun and quietly devolved into a regional backwater. But its past is neatly embodied in the Hurare Duare, a Meditteranean palace that would be more in place along the banks of a Venetian canal than by the jungle-bounded Hooghly. It is a huge, strange place but, as a Hindu temple set in the American Midwest is a window on an exotic world, so the Hurare Duare attracts the dreamers of Indian society.

The palace and its grounds stretch out for almost a kilometer on the east bank of the river. The colonnaded passageways are haunted by shouting children and the parched brown lawns are taken over by frenzied games of cricket.

Along the river runs a boardwalk and a set of ghats. I was there on a weekend and the steps were bristling with religious bathers. This is after all the Ganga.

Looking at a map this may be hard to justify but to Hindus the Hooghly channel, not the much larger Padma River, is considered the true Ganga. The orthodox defence of this anomaly is that during Vedic times the river's main course was in this direction. Another reason is that in Bangladesh, where the deltas of the Ganga and Brahmaputra mesh, the river becomes so convoluted and ethereal that the idea of a distinct Ganga is impossible. The Hooghly has a single course until it is past Calcutta and therefore it is simpler to apply the geographical myths.

For Hinduism this is significant, because India is a narrative landscape. With a multitude of languages and cultures coming together under the banner of a single religion there has to be some means to connect 700 million vastly disparate Hindus. The simplest, strongest bond is the land itself. It is the countless myths and legends directly associated with Mother India that hold Hinduism's anarchic diaspora together. Myth and landscape — this is the inextricable matrix that has become the glue of Hindustan, and the Ganga is the most encompassing aspect of that landscape. The holy waters have become, through their association with purity and compassion, the definition of the land.

Crossing the Hooghly on the small ferry between the towns of Navidweep and Mayapur I watched as milkmen dipped their cups overboard and drank directly from the milk chocolate colored water. The drops remaining in the steel cups were sprinkled into galvanized milk containers. Thus the milk of the mother cow mingled with the milk of the goddess. They all smiled at my inquisitive stares and offered me a sip, but my faith was not as strong as their stomachs.

I had come to Mayapur to see the world headquarters of the International Society for Krishna Consciousness (ISKON), the organization also known as the Hare Krishnas. What I found was a theme park on the Ganga.

Within its compound a gargantuan five-story concrete lotus housed a single flower garland. Devoted elephants ate peanuts and trumpeted mantras to Krishna. Frolicking cherubs from Italy and Brazil danced through Victorian rose gardens. Prayer ceremonies in the main temple turned into blissed-out rock concerts. And through it all wandered western devotees with distant smiles and 100,000 ogling Bengali tourists a week.

The unearthly facade of the place turned surreal when I was proudly told that at Mayapur the Hare Krishnas were going to build the largest single religious building in the world. It was to be as large as the entire Vatican City, and to function in Bengal's paddy field soils it would require a revolutionary high tech, floating foundation. It would be a $200 million behemoth in the heart of village India.

I was impressed by the ISKON complex's cleanliness and organization. It was the cleanest place that I'd visited along the river, but this only heightened its separation from the surrounding villages. The residents warned me not to go out after dark, saying, "It's dangerous out there."

The devotees, the majority of whom were westerners, were like the compound itself, clean, chatty and a little paranoid. Adi-guru, a pleasant disciple from London, attached himself to me and took on the responsibility of personal guide for my travels through the space that had become the center of his universe.

His existence centered around Krishna and how to venerate him. But Adi-guru had a soft spot for Ganga-mai and when he realized my interest he quoted a relevant passage from the Srimad Bhagavatum: "Oh king, the rivers are the veins of the gigantic body, the trees are the hairs of the body and the omnipotent air is the breath."

He went on to tell me how his denominaton revered the river as an accidentally spilt drop of the causal ocean, the fabric upon which all reality rides. Ganga was a window onto the universe's most base component.

I liked the image and Adi-guru went on to tell about the local relationship between Ganga and Krishna. In the previous rainy season the river had overrun her banks and in a week she had risen to flood the entire area. The river kept rising into the compound, inundating the grounds and putting the lower buildings underwater. Despite their ardent prayers she kept moving upwards until eventually she touched the toe of the magnificent central Krishna image in the main hall. At that point she ceased her lapping rise and slowly returned to her normal course.

Adi-guru recounted the story with gooey eyes and an inebriated smile. "Ganga-mai only wanted to touch the feet of her heavenly source," he said. Krishna is the epitome of manly love, and for Adi-guru it was only fitting that Ganga would want to be with her male counterpart.

Kali, the bringer of death, is the namesake goddess of Calcutta and it is from the little toe of her right foot that the fourth largest city in the world has grown. Legend has it that Kali was the wife of Shiva and when she died the god was so upset that he took her body on his shoulders and danced a cosmic dervish dance around the globe. But with each step his deathly waltz became more and more violent. The rest of the gods were worried that Shiva would destroy the entire world and so Vishnu, knowing that the Lord of Death would not stop his mourning dance until the body had disappeared, took a knife and threw it at the corpse. The knife sliced Kali into fifty-two pieces and these fragments of the goddess exploded across the Hindu world. It was on the western shore of a great river in Bengal that the little toe of the goddess landed. There the local fishers built a temple and they called it Kalikata.

The British first arrived at Kalikata in 1690. From the fishing village's assortment of bamboo shacks they established their first subcontinental trading post and out of that initial array of jute warehouses a city was born. The village's name was anglicized to Calcutta and the fishing hamlet grew to become the jewel of an empire upon which the sun never set.

Kalikata, the bathing area of the dark, blood hungry goddess, still exists today, but the Hooghly's waters have removed themselves to the west and the city center has shifted north. The temple that was the backbone of the great city is now trapped in a landlocked suburb, crowded on all sides by a tight assortment of concrete blocks and old mansions.

When I arrived at what is now know as Kali-ghat, the streets were shimmering black wet from a sunrise rain. The sky was overcast and a spring chill held in the air.

The neighborhood is dominated by the temple dedicated to the Goddess and on the road leading to it Hindu trinket shops were clattering open their steel shutters for the day. On the display stands lining the street the storekeepers were laying out the brass and copper accessories to the rituals of religion. Esoterically adorned statues and abstract images lay beside brightly colored packages of incense and framed pictures of the Hindu pantheon.

The way was lined with groggy-eyed beggars just arriving from their alleyway sleeping places. In India, where charity is an intrinsic part of life, the invalids lining the route to any temple are an unavoidable fixture. They align themselves in an orderly fashion, the legless and the armless mixing with the lepers and the victims of industrial accidents. They form moaning lines of rag-clad corpses, their unwashed bodies distancing them from the purity obsessed Hindu masses.

Initially their appearance is disconcerting. For westerners used to having the ugliness of the world placed behind closed doors it is a shock to see people's physical woes so openly displayed. However, after visiting a dozen or so Hindu temples, you begin to realize that the beggars are statements, reminders of what we, the physically blessed, possess. The Indian temple's boulevard of cripples is a conscious reminder of the gifts the healthy have been deeded.

The Kali temple is not as large as imagination might have it. The spiritual focus of Calcutta is only fifty meters square. The main sanctum sits to one side of a walled compound and is encircled by a marble walkway that's been worn concave by the circumambulations of the faithful.

I rounded the shrine room and walked to the sacrificial compound on the opposite side of the complex. Between those four low earthen walls Kali's blood thirst was satisfied. In a twisting line that wound out past the rear entrance, sacrificial goats and their "sponsor" families awaited the moment of deliverance. Inside the area the priests who perform the sacrifices stood, chatted, and drank ubiquitous cups of tea. For them death was a profession.

I returned to the far side of the compound and circled the temple again, marveling in one of its corners as flower garland salesmen and their customers haggled over costs. The merchants vehemently argued that they couldn't drop their prices because the purchasing money, not the marigolds, was the offering to Kali. In the business of religion there was no such thing as a sale.

I passed people relaxing on the temple steps, a young couple talking tenderly to each other, a Shiva lingam adorned with fresh cut blooms, and then arrived again at the sacrifice ground. Fresh blood soaked the marble. The day's worship had begun.

Another goat was brought in. Held by its forelegs it gave no resistance. Had it already submitted to Kali? The animal was placed neck first into a guillotine rack, its head held in place by a pin behind the skull. A boy in a black motorbike jacket, next to the goat in shock, held aloft the traditional supplementary offering to Kali, a large bottle of whiskey.

Meat and alcohol, the two things abhorred by the orthodox, become for the followers of Hindu Tantra's "left handed path" the offerings of preference.

The pujari, wearing a fresh cotton dhoti, his wide fleshy back spilling out over the material, lifted a scimitar-like axe and dropped it without effort onto the still goat. The head fell from the body in a surgical separation. No oohs or aahs rose from the crowd, for this was merely the severing of another head, an action characterized by an executioner's economy of motion.

The leather jacketed boy tossed the twitching torso to one side, the legs still bucking convulsively. The head, its mouth pulled back in a menacing grimace, followed in its wake, landing noiselessly next to the body, the lips touching what had once been its teats.

The area was washed down with two expertly aimed buckets of water. I was amazed at the coagulating speed of the animal's blood as it flowed from the compound in thick, stringy, turbid streaks.

The body was retrieved and taken outside the sanctum's iron fence where a butcher waited to skin it. The head was placed just to the left of the rear gate in a line of fresh skulls that all stared back at the execution site. It was a procession of the offered, a line of dull stares. The demonic slit-line pupils of the goats gazed blankly back into the compound, perhaps waiting for their last glimpse of Kali.

If Varanasi is the city of Shiva then Calcutta is the city of Kali. Her gruesome image is everywhere, from the simply colored paper constructions that stand out in beggar's bowls, to the over-sized, three-dimensional visions that surprise you in alleyway temples or beneath roadside bodhi trees. Calcutta thrives on her energy, benevolent until crossed, and then wrathful to the extreme.

In a city as dense and gorged as this it is impossible not to meet her dark side. Calcutta is a place where the tension hanging just below the surface is a tangible constant.

The city is a strictly segregated environment, Hindu and Muslim, Harijan and Brahmin, rich and poor. The density of the space makes it an unwritten law, and contact between the groups is cloaked in ritual until religion, money or nationalism ignites a civic explosion. Then Calcutta rocks with a malicious energy that Kali enflames.

I walked the streets at night, the pathways eerily hushed after the day's nonstop delivery of life noise. Every sidewalk rustled with the sleeptime tossing of its innumerable residents. Down each alley were repeating lines of rug shrouded bodies, a plastic bag containing their precious few belongings placed at each head. They were darkened lines of pupae, aligned symmetrically, all waiting for daylight to pull back their encasing skins.

This was home, the piece of pavement for which they pay a weekly rent. For me, to see the dream time movement of those bodies was to appreciate the adaptability of our species. To dream is to survive in Calcutta's jungle.

I walked silently, scared to wake the fidgeting masses. In one area the pavement was lit by a single flickering oil lamp at the foot of a prostrate body. The flame burned obediently, illuminating an ancient postcard of black Kali, the purveyor of dreams.

From as far back as Bhuj basa people had been telling me about the Ganga Sagar mela, and their unanimous recommendation was that if I was interested in the Ganga I had to go to the river's greatest festival.

Sagar in Hindi means ocean, so the Ganga Sagar mela therefore celebrates, at the most auspicious time of the year, the joining of the Ganga and the ocean. It is a meeting of the lifestream of India and the depthless ocean of wisdom.

When I arrived in Calcutta the city was abuzz with talk of the annual event. It can attract a quarter of a million people and Calcutta is the staging point.

The mela site is 150 kilometers south of the city on the ocean side of Sagar island. The island is deep in the heart of the Sunderbhans jungle on the southern edge of the Ganges' delta. It is an area known for swimming tigers and waterborne snakes, inhospitable territory that is little visited beyond the festival time.

The day before the festival I took advantage of the many buses and ferries that the city authorities reroute to the south, and in downtown Calcutta boarded a bus jammed with pilgrims. It was a shiny new model of the archetypal bare-boned Indian people transporter. The exterior was unstained by beetle nut juice or passengers' vomit and the interior still possessed floorboards and vinyl on the seats. But there was none of that new car odor — it was overpowered by the scent of seventy sweatily expectant humans.

Soon after takeoff it became apparent that the driver had every intention of pushing his glimmering stallion to the edge of its capabilities. Although his finish line was nowhere in sight he weaved across the road like a slalom racer, as if bullock carts and elephants had become his race gates.

I made hanging onto the safety straps swaying from the ceiling a religious act and was glad that the bodies in front of me blocked the view of the road ahead. The bus ride became an act of faith. Everyone on board had to trust that our arrival at Ganga Sagar was preordained.

We arrived, not soon enough, at Harwood Point, the terminus for the ferry ride across the Hooghly to the northern tip of Sagar island. There the bus expelled its agitated load like the contents of a contracted stomach and we joined a snaking lineup of people waiting for space on one of the boats.

Eventually we boarded a low, wide-bodied launch, the gunwales of which dropped closer to the water with every passenger it took on. By the time we left the dock people were hanging from the outside railings and the water line was inches from the deck.

My shipmates were of the ecstatically delirious denomination and our thirty minute passage was occupied with loud mantras and prayers that everyone but me had memorized in childhood. At different intervals old ladies would rise from the open benches and muscle their way to the railings to toss offerings of money and food to the river. In the sardine can atmosphere of the ferry I was impressed by the ladies' determination. The movement involved more devotion than the offering itself.

It was on the barge that I was able to appreciate the Ganges' delta. At river level her waters glint from every corner of the horizon. There land is the non-element. In the delta the water pushes all its boundaries. The solid earth is a mass to be manipulated. In the delta the Goddess Ganga has cloned herself so immeasurably that her motives come into question. Is she postponing her final mergence with the ocean?

In the slowing of her current and her domination of the physical landscape the river becomes a divine mirror on the human psyche. Hindu masters talk of the final acceptance as being the most difficult. It is the loss of life, the annihilation of the body that we have grown accustomed to. For humans it is a struggle to enter that void, while for the Ganga there may be hesitation, but there is also inevitability. She moves to a higher plane with what Shanti-mai described as "Grace."

Reaching the island side I once again joined the convulsive flow of the faithful. We were herded towards a temporary bus park by stick wielding event organizers. The dust blown square, bordered on one side by the sea and the other by jungle, was a battleground for the devout. Every bus that rolled in was the scene of a tiny war. With each arrival scores of pilgrims, frantic to traverse the last twenty-five kilometers, would swarm onto the vehicle like ants over a block of cheese. The bus conductors would rip the clinging bodies from the flanks and roof and throw them to the ground. Arguments erupted in the name of the Ganga but they were drowned by the explosive roar of the deep-throated diesels and the scream of air horns.

My ardor for the goddess was not as fervent as that of my colleagues and I decided to wait out the delirium, hoping to catch a lull in the waves of pilgrims and a less crowded bus.

My chance came a few hours later when a single exhausted bus spluttered in and a dozen people and myself made a dash for it. We secured seats, but almost simultaneously another bloated ferry disgorged its passengers. They made a frantic rush towards us. Within seconds the vehicle was jammed to bursting and the sagging bus pulled ever so slowly out of the park.

A crowd chased us, making leaps of faith at any available grip on the vehicle. On the roof the conductor, clambering like Spiderman around the bus's outer skin, remorselessly tossed bodies to the dirt. Life and limb were of secondary concern, and the only goal was to reach Ganga Sagar by sunrise.

I heard the conductor's whistle. He must have cleared the frame of excess human baggage, and the vehicle went up through the gears. I had presumed that with this kind of a load the driver would want to ease his way through the final leg but within minutes the palm trees outside were hurtling by with disconcerting speed, while inside the passengers moaned as if trapped on a storm ridden ship.

Another hour and the mela ground was upon us. There we were unceremoniously ejected.

We had been dropped two kilometers from the water's edge and even at that distance from the beach the scene was a beehive of activity.

"Mela, Mela, Mela, all India is a mela, my friend," Raj Chatterjee had told me.

Ganga Sagar was Hindustan in microcosm. As I made my way to the ocean I could make out all manner of costume: saris, dhotis, kurtas, lungis, Salwar khamiz, and three-piece suits. Pilgrims from every corner of India in every conceivable cloth from torn cotton to the finest silks had gathered on the Bengali beach.

The middle class were there in mismatched polyester, and the rich appeared, tracked and trailed by bevies of peons, but the bulk of the crowds were simple rural folk. For all the differences what was striking was that everyone had come as a single pulsing body, beholden only to the mother. The river had brought these people here and joined them into a single obsequious mass.

I was surprised that, after the troubles of getting there, at the mela ground I never felt jammed or pressured. The crowd imitated the river, an entity in constant motion.

People moved, others watched, the beggars supplicated with a smile, a little girl in dreadlocks shouted, "Halloo!" while a withered old woman offered me a banana and a majestic grandmother was carried to the water's edge in a bamboo palanquin. Hundreds of thousands of stories were all brought to one conclusion, all released to the one entity that would listen, the river.

At the tide's edge I stood barefoot, staring at a horizon moving to morning. The water reflected the sky's first fire of sunrise and thirty meters out from the beach an old couple called to me, "Aiye, Aiye." Come, Come.

I waded out into the thigh-deep water. The man, a head shorter than myself, bid me welcome, and his wife, whose wet sari clung to her matronly figure, smiled. The man put his arm around my shoulder, holding me close like a child to be comforted. His wife faced us and dipped her cupped hands into the water. She lifted them to our lowered heads, letting the mother's water fall on us as she chanted, "Jai Ganga Hai!"

The water was cool and my skin tingled. Through the small cascade before my eyes, I could see the far-off golden sun stroking the watery line at the edge of the earth. Ganga and Surya, the river and the sun, were ever so gently moving together; the water and the light, wisdom and energy, were touching. It was the kiss of life.

Rhein/Rhine/Rijn

Lake Thoma is a pristine pool of the coolest, darkest water imaginable. Guarded on three sides by snow-checkered peaks, its open edge gazes out over a narrow, twisting furrow that winds off into the undulating mountain sea of the central Alps. This is the valley of the infant Rhine.

I had arrived just before evening after climbing the Oberalp Pass by bicycle and then following a foot trail south to the lake. Snow had clung to the path, and in some places my feet had given way. Two couples had passed me on their way down, both pairs staring, possibly debating the sanity of one heading for the lake so late in the day. But I continued on, the source pulling me upwards with its own gravity, and an hour after leaving the road I found myself entering the narrow cirque that cradled the wellspring. I was alone, and my arrival was rewarded with unpeopled silence. There was only myself and the birth of Europe's greatest river.

The lake itself is small, 150 meters by 50 meters, and the end close to the exit was gaining a translucent cover of spiderwebbed ice, evidence of the coming winter. The opposite extremity held a delta in miniature, the result of two source streams originating high up in the northern couloir. In the freezing air the creeks spread themselves across the ridge and in the falling light set the slope ablaze. It was a hillside shimmering with a crystal veneer. I let my eyes follow the waters up to the horizon, to a space that was obscured by rock and cloud, to the point of the Rhine's true origin, the heavens.

The sun was sneaking behind the mountain to the south, its waning reflection caught in the still, black waters and as it was pulled from sight, a sweeping shadow moved across the surface of the pond. In that silvery atmosphere, surrounded by crisp echoes and touched by the cold kiss of a mountain night, you could understand the ancestry of the Rhine's name. "Rein" in German means "the pure."

The tiny watershed had an air of quiet beginnings. I wandered along the trail following the tarn's northern shore and found a bronze plaque set into the cliff wall. Its inscription read, "Rhein Quelle," the source of the Rhine. But for me the plate was an absurd overstatement. In a space that was so inundated with the essence of birth the plaque was a symptom of man's need to label and categorize. Feelings were being overridden by facts.

Yet the sense of beginnings that I had that day was a result of more than just my proximity to the source of the Rhine, because the Andermatt/Oberalp Mountains are the calving grounds for a set of Europe's most important rivers. The area has been described as the hub of the continent because from this central point radiate out a series of the region's definitive flows. To the south runs the Ticino which, after a sojourn in Lago Maggiore, will become the Po and water the fertile plains of northern Italy. To the west flows the Rhone, the irrigator of central France's wine and grains. To the north issues the Reuss, the lifeblood of the Swiss central plateau, which, after merging with the Aare and Limmat rivers, will join the Rhine at Waldshut. Finally, to the east, emanates the Rhine itself, untamed in its youth but swiftly becoming the patriarch flow of Northern Europe.

It was hard to believe that tiny Lake Thoma, that thin shard of blue on the gray-green face of Europa, was the starting point of the river that becomes the definitive line of geography for the Germanic world. The Rhine is not just the inspiration for the Central European identity, but, in a practical sense, is the fluid infrastructure of the nations it traverses. Thirty-one million people draw their drinking water from the Rhine and its tributaries; it irrigates thousands of hectares of the most fertile farmland in the six nations it passes through, and, in a sad sideline to modernity, it has become the industrial sewer for a handful of the world's greatest powers.

On that blissful evening I sat looking across the pond, relishing the place's feeling of pure beginnings, and then, when the sun had completely left the meadow, I turned back for the pass. But as I crossed the lip of the lake's out-stream my reverie was broken. Below I could see the winding switchback curves of Hauptstrasse 19, and roaring along it, utilizing the highway's banked corners and extra wide 180 degree turns, were a pair of German sports cars.

A Mercedes and a Porsche were battling upwards in an all out race. The scream of quick-shifted gears and engines pushed to the red zone reverberated around the valley. They dueled back and forth, supremacy measured in centimeters, noise the evidence of their triumph, and then, in a synchronous hop in gears, they topped the summit and were lost from view.

Even after the cars disappeared, I could still hear their engines throwing insolent vibrations off the hills. It was a rude awakening and an initiation into what was to become a recurring theme of my travels on the Rhine. It has become for many of the people who inhabit its shores merely a background landscape.

But maybe that initiation had come earlier in the day. On my climb up to the pass I had heard the metallic click, click of a bicycle chain and turned to see another cyclist gaining on me. He pulled alongside and breathlessly introduced himself.

Albert Geicher was a railway worker out for an afternoon ride. He was a large man whose belly was barely restrained by his tight lycra one-piece suit. His thighs were those of a bull, massive and meaty, and his balding head was wrapped in a pair of silver sunglasses that gave him the look of a gargantuan fly. Albert was a jovial man, inquisitive about my plans and, when I related that I was following the Rhine, he proved to be an encyclopedia of Rheinisch knowledge.

Albert admitted his fascination with the river, but it was an interest in the logic and engineering of the flow. When I asked him about the river's myths and history, he said, "Bhah, a river is a river, it is up to us to use it. Ja?"

He had kayaked and rafted on it, ridden and driven along its banks, drunk its waters, and used it for irrigation, but as an entity worthy of introspective or spiritual attention it had been removed from his psyche. According to Albert the Rhine had been tamed and made "useful."

The river for him was useful for purely economic or recreational purposes. His fascination and respect for the river lay in his knowledge of how difficult it had been to "tame" and how much resultant power was created. In order to appreciate its modern, pragmatic persona, Albert had subverted the river's role in his own Germanic makeup.

Later that evening, walking back down to the Oberalp trailhead, I caught up with a hunter, a clean-cut version of the North American weekend warrior. He was dressed in immaculate jager wool, complete with a feathered hat, and was trailed by a trio of well-behaved hunting dogs. His gun, slung over his right shoulder, had the burnished gleam of a well-tended tool. As he ambled down the trail he whistled an Alpine tune, halfway between a folksong and a military march.

I surprised him, and he stopped in his tracks addressing me abruptly in Romansch, the Latin based tongue indigenous to the area. I indicated my lack of comprehension and he relaxed. We traded some phrases in English, but it was obvious he was a man of few words. When I inquired whether he had managed to bag any birds he guffawed, shook his head, and said with a heavy accent, "Na! Here I don't think there is any game now, too many people, not enough space." The Oberalp is one of the most remote areas in the Alps, but I had to agree with his statement. Less than a kilometer away a tour bus roared up the pass with a dozen bobbing heads peeking out from behind pink curtains.

At the trailhead he had me tend to his dogs while he went to fetch his truck from the parking lot at the summit chalet. The dogs were ecstatic to have a new handler and covered me in wet kisses. Their master soon returned driving a khaki green Mercedes 4x4 that matched his outfit. With a stiff handshake and a solemn face he retrieved his hounds and loaded them into the blanket covered rear space. Then he pulled out onto the pavement through crunchy old snow, and with a squeal of his tires returned to his hunting lodge.

I pitched my tent believing that I was now alone, but as I prepared dinner in the shelter's tiny vestibule I felt the ground beneath me rumble and then perceptibly shake.

I rushed out expecting an earthquake to rip open the ground before me, but was struck by a 10,000 watt halogen spotlight bearing down on my camp. Something immense was making directly for me. In that split second I was without an answer and as I waited for the inevitable, time had no past or future.

Then, just as suddenly, the beam disappeared. The vibration coursed directly beneath my feet and the roar followed in its wake. I realized that I was camped on the grassed-over roof of the Oberalp railway tunnel.

The next morning I was up with the sun. Once on my bike I rolled down out of the heavens, feeling the road's curves unfurl beneath my wheels. It was early fall and the mountainsides had transformed their multifarious summer greens to an outburst of rusts and golds, russets and reds.

Just above the first settlement I rejoined the treeline. Tsamutch is a true Swiss alpine village with huge, painstakingly finished chalets and a single laned road flanked by a cobblestone sidewalk.

But the village's storybook facade was offset by the unnaturally uniform terrain and color of the golf course constructed just below it. Barely two hundred meters below the forest's altitudinal limit some alpine entrepreneur had developed his dream. Meticulously manicured, the course was a tight mountain par three rather than an expansive coastal links.

The nascent Rhine had been redirected to water what is the sub-alpine pasture's newest incarnation. The development's otherworldliness struck me as evidence more of the possibility of engineering in the landscape than the potential of sport. In the bright light of that cool autumn morning there was no one indulging in a round. It was a deserted oasis of the recreation age.

The road drew me down. A fairytale alpine landscape unfolded by the path — smiling cows, their teats full of cheesy milk; chateaux with long sweeping roof lines draped in blooming flowers; fields, green and thick with alpine grass; and below, the Rhine, caught in its steep-walled gorge, reflecting subtle hints of the late morning sun. Beside me people were busy, toiling energetically with whatever was at hand, not concerned with my comings and goings.

Disentis is the first substantial town on the river's course. I stopped to admire the Benedictine monastery, reputed to be the oldest in the country. The cloister glowed in the morning light, its roof steaming with sun-shocked dew. It was a monument to the doctrines that had for centuries ruled the lives of the valley's dwellers.

It was a huge edifice that, in its day, must have been a considerable tribute to the power of Christianity. The complex's massive scale was out of context with the small population of the Surselva valley. But I was not surprised, seeing it as a credit to the creative energy of a young river. Like the saddhus of Gangotri, the monastery's founding monks must have also felt the river's inspiration and the lives of those pioneer brothers had inspired the thousands who had followed them to that high valley in search of greater wisdom.

Farther on I came to Flims, a contemporary monument to a new religion — tourism.

Flims is an interesting mix of old and new. Ancient log barns, twisted with time, sit in pastures before stucco-clad Mediterranean style condos. On newly harvested fields farmers sprayed reeking fertilizer that splattered on the nearby pavement and soiled the finish of passing Mercedes. It was a town teeming with shiny sport utility vehicles, flashy full suspension mountain bikes and more patisseries than a small city. These to me, were signs of the athletic rich, people with enough money to take time off work but too occupied to laze around on a beach.

Flims, until the end of the last century, had been one of the many forgotten villages in the central Alps, a remote hamlet far removed from the traditional north-south trade routes.

The valley's residents were martyrs to climate and altitude. It was a land steeped in religion and faith, the people devoted to ritual and dependent on God's good tidings. The Christian God was the great clockmaker who controlled the flow of the Vorderrhein and the cycle of the seasons. For the god-fearing Flimsers the product of the harvest was dependent upon their religious devotion.

But the discovery by the urban romantics in the late nineteenth century of the Alpine landscape's unspoiled form attracted the first tourists to the Surselva region. The movement was for decades confined to the wealthy elite, but in the 1950s and '60s, with the gentrification of alpine skiing, tourism became a booming industry. Fun, adventure and the pursuit of happiness. Flims moved from a rural backwater to a stop on the media circus of the world cup ski circuit. In less than a hundred years it had moved from obscurity to global recognition.

I sat in a field eating bread and cheese; across from me stood a line of unfortunately similar hotels. At my back an inquisitive cow, from whose neck swung a huge brass bell, leant over an electric fence to get a better look at my lunch. People with beautifully coifed hair, shopped at boutiques stocked with the latest "active fashions." Overhead a helicopter slung a triangualated piece of a ski lift tower to some distant high altitude construction site. Had man actually improved the land-scape, or was alpine tourism just another superficial pressure vent for an exploding population?

From Flims the highway climbs to the village of Trin and then starts a steep descent into the Alpenrhein valley. It was on that stretch of road that I was the most scared that I've ever been in Europe. Forget London night club bouncers, or skinheads in Berlin. The road from Flims to Chur is so jammed with traffic that it is impossible for a two-wheeled traveler to feel safe. On one side is a sheer drop to the valley, while on the other white-knuckled drivers engulfed by road rage are too possessed to notice a single cyclist. It is a road that I will not be return-ing to soon.

Motorized traffic is one of the major contributors to the Alps envi-ronmental demise. The construction of roads slices the landscape into an asphalt matrix, diverts streams and rivers and then cuts away at the mountains themselves. At altitude the pollution and noise of internal combustion engines is exponentially destructive. The thin air reverberates with the rumble of juggernaut trucks and the air fills with thick clouds of diesel exhaust. Traffic is in fact one of the major stumbling blocks in Switzerland's political links with the European Union. The Swiss do not want to accommodate a dramatic increase in transalpine traffic.

At Reichenau at the outlet of the Surselva valley, the Vorderrhein and the Hinterrhein fuse, and there the Alpenrhein is born. The Vorderrhein is the "frontal" river that I had followed from the Oberalp, while the Hinterrhein, the Rhine's other source stream flows south from the San Bernadino Pass. The debate as to which is the true source has been raging for centuries to no avail. The two are equal in their primacy, which is fitting, as Switzerland bills itself as a birthplace of democracy.

The forested hill above Reichenau is dominated by a church and a castle, the twin powers of historical Europe. The village marks the start of one of Europe's oldest transalpine trade routes. Moving up the Rhine and down the Moesa valley, it has been used from before the time of the Romans to move between the Italian peninsula and central Europe.

Intensive trade began in the fifteenth century with the development of plank technology, the insertion of heavy timbers into the impassable sections of the Vorderrhein gorge. With the construction through the canyon of a permanent path named the Via Malla, literally the "evil road," the route became an all season thoroughfare.

The castles that dot the local hillsides highlight the Rhine trade route's importance as an historical source of income for the aristocracy. By exacting a stiff tariff on goods traversing their fiefdoms, the robber princes grew rich without the benefit of vast lands.

The need to protect the route and its revenue, especially from the Hapsburg nobility to the north, is one of the main reasons that brought the Canton of Grisons, through which the road travels, into the Swiss confederation.

The original Via Malla has been buried by a six-lane international freeway, and the sound of snorting mules has been replaced by the roar of multitrailered transports. But with the advent of ever faster communications the cosmopolitan economy of the area has grown dramatically.

The area to the north of the confluence is a peculiarly industrialized zone. For its entire length to the Bodensee the river is lined with cubist styled factories that appear haphazardly scattered through farmers' fields. In fact, the first sight that accosts you at the beginnings of the consolidated Rhine is the mammoth E.M.S. factory, a steam belching behemoth producing plastics and polymers to be exported worldwide.

The Alpenrhein is a productive collision point for the Germanic world. Austria, Leichenstein, Germany, and Switzerland mingle along this stretch of the river, and although it may appear far removed on a map, it has, through the industry of its inhabitants, become one of the wealthiest regions of Europe.

The Vorarlberg district of Austria is the fastest growing province in the country. St. Gallen Canton in Switzerland is part of the industrial heartland of the Swiss Central Plateau, while Baden-Wurtenburg is the home to much of Germany's auto and aircraft industry, and Leichenstein, the tiny 160 square kilometer principality, is a banking and financial haven known the world over.

I neared the Swiss-Leichenstein border late in the day. The light was leaving the valley, and as I rolled down the hill to the unguarded frontier I began to notice incongruous shadowy shapes off in the trees. I slowed down and stopped. Surprised I realized that the amorphous outlines inside the forest's shade-line were dozens of tanks, artillery pieces, trucks and jeeps, all sitting under camouflage netting.

A little farther on I saw heavy bunkers dug into the earth, their concrete turrets painted the same shade as the surrounding forest. Tank traps were overgrown with vines, and fatigue-clad soldiers, bearing heavy weapons, lounged inside the shadows.

It looked as if a war was about to erupt on that forgotten border. But what I was seeing was evidence of the world's most militarized nation. Switzerland the neutral is also Switzerland the armed. In a population of seven million, the military, the vast majority of whom are part-time soldiers, numbers 400,000. The army is a "war deterrent," in existence to protect the country's neutrality.

The Rhine, which forms over a quarter of the nation's border, is an integral part of Switzerland's defense policy. The river is a boundary between "us and them," even if "them" is the Teutonic fatherland to the north.

Constantly along its shores I saw evidence of its military importance — bunkers on the wooded embankments, barbed wire by the roadside, and soldiers in neat, green woolens pacing riverside paths with matte black automatic weapons. Both banks looked identical and yet the presence of such nationalistic artifacts created a more than geographic separation between those two.

At Reichenau the river finally turns north. Its descent, over 1,800 meters in the previous seventy kilometers, slows radically and after emerging from between Rätikon Ridge and the Glarus Alps, the flow becomes noticeably more docile and meandering. It is along the border with Leichenstein that the effects of what Albert Geicher might have called the river's "taming" become apparent.

From as early as 1812 plans for the "redirection" of the Alpenrhein had been drawn, and from 1895 to the present work has continued. The aim of the project has been to straighten the river's course and thus increase the amount of farmland along its banks. In the tradition of Victorian efficiency the engineers wanted to transform the marshy delta area into the agricultural centerpiece of the valley. But dehydrating the boggy wetlands caused the irretrievable loss of species, the water table dropped and the increased flow of the river caused serious erosion even farther back up the Alpenrhein. The full consequences of actions initiated 150 years ago are only now starting to be known.

I was guided through the Austrian part of the delta by my old friend Rochus Schertler, a jovial bear of a man and a research assistant at the Dornbirn Nature Museum. Rochus pointed out the plethora of botanical changes that had resulted from the soil's dehydration, but he also pointed out that the "domestication" of the Alpenrhein and its effects were only part of a chain of human initiated alterations. The valley has changed constantly with habitation, and the species that have been lost are not always indigenous. The work of conservationists in Vorarlberg was in ethno-cultural rather than wilderness preservation. In Rochus' words, "There is no wilderness here; everything has been touched by man. Our job is to be able to preserve some of the stages of those changes."

It is impossible not to change the environments that we live in. The point for Rochus was that the goal of the environmentally aware is to be conscious of their effect on the land and to minimize the resulting changes.

A day later, and with beautiful weather, Rochus took me to the Rappenlochschlucht, the gorge of the Dornbirner Ach, a small river that exits into the Bodensee only a few hundred meters east of the Rhine. We rode our bikes through glistening wet forest to the base of the trail and then walked upwards on a path cut directly into the wall of the canyon. The rock, where it wasn't covered in dewy lichens, was cool to touch and in places wide-capped mushrooms poked up through the thin moss.

We reached the gorge just as the noon sun hung directly overhead and were graced with the sight of that rare moment when light illuminates the canyon's deepest recesses. The moist cavity steamed with the unexpected heat, and the golden autumn leafed trees at the far end of the passage were doused in a midday, fairytale mist. We stopped to appreciate it, and with our recognition, the moment passed and the scene dissolved again into shade.

But the Rappenloch's place in history has not, unfortunately, been secured by its beauty. It is exceptional by being the first hydroelectric project in Austria. It was here in 1886 that textile magnate F.M. Hammerle initiated a hydrostation that was to alter forever the Vorarlberger's concept of rivers. Water became synonomous with power.

With its opening by Kaiser Franz Joseph the plant became a symbol for the rapid industrialization of the district. The one small power plant became a catalyst for the evolution of the Alpenrhein into a center of the world's textile markets.

The station is still in operation today, and the static hum of the turbines resonates around the little meadow on which it is set. A thin, graveled road leads up to it, so small that new generators have to be delivered piece by piece. It is history and it looks the part, housed in an Alpen manor whose top floor is inhabited by a caretaker family. Off the balcony fell a rainbow of meadow flowers, from behind which a German shepherd eyed me warily.

I left the Alpenrhein valley a few days later, riding back out to the delta and following the Bodensee coastline west. At the Swiss-Austrian frontier I was greeted by two smartly dressed border guards, and with no questions was ushered back into Switzerland. I turned north, past the money changers and cheap booze boutiques that populate all international boundaries, and followed the trail along the river.

I traced the old Rhine towards Rorschach and found the bicycle path that circumnavigates the lake. It is a pleasant combination of backroads, walking trails and utilitarian connectors, and the perfect way to see Europe's second largest lake.

The Bodensee, named for Bodomia, the royal palace erected on its northern shores, is known as Lake Constance to the Swiss and has been described as the world's largest bathtub. The Rhine is its plumbing, filling it from the south and draining it to the west. Unfortunately this celestial piping results in twenty meters of the surface area being lost to the deposited sediments every year. The Bodensee is destined to disappear from view in twelve thousand years.

Nowadays the lake is known for its tourist attractions. As I circled it I was shocked by the number of caravans, trailers, cottages and marinas. The lake is a playground for the masses, but I also saw it as a modern myth. The tourists are pilgrims of the industrial age, attracted, like their ancestors, to the recuperative properties of water. The sound of water outside a cabin door and the wave of relaxation as the river wraps around a bather are just interpretations of ancient mythology's thoughts on the river's power.

But it was late October, well past the tourist season, and the lake was lashed by a mountain wind that drove its surface into whitecapped fits. I liked the human quiet of the off-season. It felt as if, when freed from the roar of race boats and the whine of jetskis, the lake was again able to take on its true character.

The bike path was constantly paralleled by train tracks to my left, a consistent hundred meters from the water, and until Rorschach, where the mainline veered south to Saint Gallen, my contemplations were visited frequently by the rumble of tightly scheduled trains. Rail grades have, through necessity, imitated the route of water. Water naturally follows the path of least resistance through a landscape, so, in the tradition of the ancient trade routes, train tracks and highways moved with it. The routes that we now travel would have been inconceivable without the river to guide the way.

Strangely though, with the nineteenth century's transition from a water based canal transport system to a land based one of rails and roads, the river was transformed from a medium to an impediment. Watercourses were entities to be crossed and forded, obstacles in the push to connect a continent. Bridges became the epitome of the engineer's endeavors, marvels of the new age, temples to the church of logic. The simplified crossing of a river meant to a great extent that the river as a piece of landscape was forgotten. Today it is only when we hear of floods and their destruction that we can have an inkling of our ancestors' respect for water's physical power. We have lost touch with the river as a necessary danger in everyday travels.

Romanshorn — I loved that name — is set on a literal horn of land that I dreamed must have been settled by the ever aggressive Romans. I was wrong. The town was first mentioned in 779 and owed its importance to its easily accessible location at the end of the valley that led to Winterthur and Zurich. The railway reached it in 1855, and by 1911 the harbor was handling 80,000 freight cars a year.

But time has changed Romanshorn. Rivers and rails have been eclipsed by the road, and in 1976 the rail ferry service across the lake was discontinued. The town's warehouses and holding yards now lie silent, possibly waiting for some developer to metamorphose them into a more timely incarnation, tourist condos perhaps.

However, not far from Romanshorn I had an encounter with the man most associated with the renaissance of thought towards the river and its subconscious powers. It was in the village of Kesswill that the psychoanalyst C.G. Jung was born in 1875. Soon after he moved to Laufen, by the Rhine falls, but his childhood spent by the water undoubtedly had an effect on his later thoughts and writings. He said that some of his earliest memories were of the river and the spectacular power of the Rhine falls. He declared that when he traveled with his mother to visit family on Lake Constance "I could not be dragged away from the water. The lake stretched away into the distance. This expanse of water was an inconceivable pleasure to me."

Jung's first encounter with death was related to the river. A body was retrieved from the Rhine by fishermen and although they obstructed him from seeing it, he had no doubt that what had occurred was of great importance. Pleasure and finality — the river bracketed so much that the doctor was contemplating. It was impossible for Jung to dissociate himself from the river, and it became one of the elementary symbols of the unconscious upon which he based his theories.

From Romanshorn it was on to Munsterlingen, a town known for the Bendictine convent built above it. In its abbey sits a bust of Saint John the Evangelist, a statue that is transferred between the nunnery and the cloister in the town of Hague, twenty-five kilometers north across the lake. The bust is shifted between the towns every time the lake is frozen deep enough to safely walk between the towns, an event known locally as the "Seegfrörne." The last such walk across the ice took place in 1963 and since then the dour face of the Saint has sat on the lake's southern shore.

But the convent is little used by the nuns these days, for the complex has been overtaken by the state and transformed into a psychiatric institution. The national apparatus has inherited from the church and its saints the welfare of those deemed unfit to care for themselves.

Another eight kilometers on and I was in Kreuzlingen, the Swiss section of Konstanz, the largest city on the Bodensee. Staying on the bike path I passed an impressive ice arena and tennis hall and on the far side of it found myself face to face with a chainlink fence that disappeared into the lake. This was the Swiss-German border. I followed the barrier back into town and found an empty customs post. No one was guarding the fatherland's frontier, so I rolled into Germany unopposed.

By crossing the border I moved into Konstanz, a venerable old city with the look of a well-polished antique. It had the feeling of a tourist destination, and I later discovered that its population doubles in the summertime. The refurbished downtown smelt of leather and perfume mingled with coffee and pastry. The rumble of shiny cobblestones rattled beneath my wheels, and in contrast to the crowds of beautifully made up shoppers thronging the arcades, I was conscious of my own pungent aroma.

Konstanz has a long history, the highlight being the four year long Council of Constance (1414-18), which was possibly the greatest gathering of the middle ages. The city, then with a population of 7,000, hosted more than 70,000 delegates from every corner of the continent. The assembly was organized by the Roman Catholic church to revitalize the rapidly deteriorating fabric of Catholicism. Konstanz was chosen because it was debatably neutral, a river principality trapped between borders.

One of the chief guests to the conference was the religious reformer Jan Hus, the precursor of Martin Luther. His theology was controversially reformist but he had come to make peace with the Roman bureaucracy. Invited under the protection of King Sigismund, Hus was given no chance to voice his ideas and was shamelessly arrested and sentenced as a heretic. He was taken to the banks of the Rhine and burnt at the stake. Needless to say, little was accomplished by the conference to quell the tide of Protestantism.

After pondering the results of the conference's four year bureaucratic nightmare, I decided that the piece of art I appreciated most in the city was Peter Lenk's "Imperia," a nine meter statue that dominates the entrance to the harbor. It is a huge revolving female figure of the most Amazonian proportions and represents the hundreds of courtesans that followed the envoys to the church council. More, I think, would have been accomplished if those working ladies had usurped the council's decision making process and implemented some pragmatism into the ailing bureaucracy.

In Konstanz I stayed in a defunct lighthouse that had been converted into a hostel. The tower stood on a hill overlooking the lake and boasted an unobstructed 360-degree panorama. The lake lay to the east as far as my eye could see, its late afternoon golden veneer disrupted by only the occasional shadowy sailboat. The wind that had pushed at my back all day had followed me to nightfall. Its gusts curled around the lighted spire, whistled through the iron banisters and squeezed in past old wooden windows. It was a constant reminder of the lake's mountain sources.

In my room I bunked with a German student called Deiter. He was a young man just starting university and his enthusiasm was infectious. He invited me out for a beer and we rode our bikes back through the nighttime streets into town.

After a few drinks at a local pub Deiter dragged me on to a dance club that gyrated with hundreds of black-lit and strobe-lit teenagers. There, with the bass beats sticking to my ribs, I swayed to a rhythm that moved like some ethereal fluid. The music rode me, ambient electronica that swept me clean and kept my body dancing beyond thoughts of tiredness. We danced late into the night conversation was impossible with the DJ's bass overwhelming the space. Everyone was absorbed in the beat. Beyond murmurs between ourselves and the music all of us were past attempts at outward communication.

On the way home, my ears still ringing, Deiter and I stopped on the bridge over the Rhine. He stood and stared at the flow, transfixed by its movement in the yellowed light of the street lamps.

"Jono," he said, "being in the river is like being in the music. It doesn't stop. You let it move over you, and through you, and it only carries you to shore when it wants to . . . I think the river and the music are the same, pure and thoughtful. I love them both."

At Konstanz the Obersee, the main body of the lake, presses into the narrow channel of the Seerhein and exits a few kilometers farther away as the Untersee. The Untersee is a much smaller lake, but that day it felt as if the wind was being funneled directly into it. On the lake, whitecaps shattered the surface and a brightly colored catamaran mirrored my frantic pace while angled up on a single hull. The breeze worked on me, transforming my back into a sail that pushed me forward ever faster.

At Ermatingen I climbed through steeply terraced vineyards to see the Arenenberg palace, the former home-in-exile of the Emperor Napoleon's family. The chateau was smaller than I expected, a simple estate house of three stories with an enviable view over to Reichenau Island on the German shore.

I imagined Napoleon III staring north across the lake on a day such as when I was there, with the wind moaning through the old house and the waves crashing on the beach. The lake, like early nineteenth-century France, would have been in turmoil, and possibly the young Napoleon envisioned himself as a latter-day Louis XIV, a sun king to pacify the storm. Borders, nationalism and the tension created by them is the modern history of the Rhine. For the Napoleonic family to be by its shores would have been a constant reminder of the ideologies they had fostered far to the north.

Stein am Rhein, another twenty kilometers farther on, is reached by a brand new white concrete bridge. The ultra-modern span, however, is a deceiving passageway, as it stretches from a well-planned contemporary Swiss village to a town that looks as if it has stepped out of the late Renaissance.

The shops and houses of the old quarter are beautiful wood and stone constructions. The heavy timber frames form intricate latticeworks, their open spaces decorated lavishly with frescoes that range from biblical scenes to the professions of the buildings' occupants. The architecture's only external submission to the twentieth century is the incongruous neon signs blinking in their windows. Here Ray-ban and Pepsi are superimposed on the Middle Ages.

Stein am Rhein's buildings, unlike their contemporaries along the Ganges, don't lean or curve with age — they are engineered to stand, straight-backed, against the ravages of time. Switzerland is the oldest nation in Europe; the 700-year-old confederation is very much a political construct, and the buildings of Stein am Rhein are some of its most important icons.

To me the town was a tribute to Swiss perfectionism, a Brigadoon evolved out of the Rheinisch mists. In Switzerland, as with every nation state, history is man-made. The multitude of refurbished town squares that I had seen were historical icons, a past made tangible through architecture.

Everything in Switzerland from engineering projects to cathedrals is dated and recorded. It is this penchant for documentation, and the country's subliminal fascination with the landscape, that has engendered this intense relationship between history, earth and construction. The Swiss have altered their difficult landscape and tamed the nature that for so long ruled them. The architectural and engineering wonders that surprise you at every turn of a Swiss road are proof of that accomplishment.

The domestication of the Rhine is one of the greatest chapters of that story. It has been weaned away from its flooding tendencies, and its flow has been managed for the benefit of human industry. Maybe the pacified Rhine is the greatest living piece of Swiss history.

Twenty-nine kilometers west and I was in Schaffhausen, a larger version of Stein am Rhein centered around another beautifully renovated city center. In its main square, not far from the river, stands an impressive statue of the Swiss national hero, William Tell. His crossbow is slung easily over his right shoulder, his full beard flows around his neck, and a look of single-minded defiance marks his face. He is the model of Swiss neutrality, a man who withstood the power of the Hapsburgs and refused to join in a larger European conflict.

Yet Schaffhausen stands out in recent history as the only town in neutral Switzerland to have been bombed by the Allies in World War Two. Official history records the bombing as an accidental drop of high explosives on the city's industrial sector. However, the mishap occurred twice, and unofficial word has it that the Allies were making a less than subtle reminder to the bureaucrats in Bern about their neutrality. Large amounts of Swiss weapons had been finding their way across the Rhine and into the hands of the German Wehrmacht. It was a piece of history that jeopardizes the legacy of William Tell, but highlights that building block modern industry, blind economics.

Four kilometers from the city center lies the feature that Schaffhausen is renowned for, the Rhine Falls. Dropping twenty-three meters across a width of 150 the Rheinfallen are the largest and most powerful waterfalls on the continent, and it is this incongruous piece of geology that explains the rise of the city's fortunes.

The lip of stone that the water charges over forms a natural barrier between the upper and lower Rhine. Thus, the prodigious amount of cargo that traversed the river from the eleventh century onwards had to be transshipped a kilometer overland between the two sections. Like the entry to the San Bernadino Pass, the falls were a bottleneck in the movement of goods, and the merchants who controlled the passage reaped the rewards. More recently, though, the falls have been the birthplace for a different type of industry.

The sight of so much moving water and the deafening roar of a rushed river makes the Rheinfallen's energy hyper-present. With the Victorian era's assumption that the natural world was something to be harnessed, the falls' undeniable strength attracted the attention of those who wanted to utilize the water's power.

Initially waterwheels and small electrical plants were built, but the first and only large scale employment of the potential was in 1888, when Allusuisse built Europe's first aluminum smelter.

To transform bauxite ore into the light metal requires vast amounts of energy. It was a refinement in the processing procedure in the late nineteenth century and the development of hydroelectricity that made the metal a commercially viable commodity. However, it is a sad statement on the endpoint of that energy that, today, crumpled aluminum foil and colorful yogurt container lids lay scattered around the monument commemorating the dismantled smelter's hundredth anniversary.

The falls personify the power of water. The processing of aluminum, with its fantastic energy requirements, and the economic power generated by the transshipment of goods are just two human byproducts of the river's infinite energy.

I stayed that night in a hostel housed in the castle that overlooks the falls from the south. It was a pleasant rustic place with thick polished stone walls, wooden planked floors and thinly mattressed bunkbeds. My only other companions were a doctor and his young son spending some "quality time" together. With the three of us sharing the same room we had an inevitably long conversation on the river, the falls and their European future.

Dr. Starck and his family lived in Mannheim, the second largest port on the Rhine. He was a cancer specialist who, along with many of his colleagues, was concerned about the quality of the drinking water drawn from the Rhine's water table. As he said, "Nothing has ever been concretely proven, but I believe that my patients' ever-increasing systemic weaknesses have a lot to do with the river's pollution."

He pointed to his son, and with Prussian briskness said, "My son for example, so many allergies and constant colds — is his immune system the same as his grandfather's?" It was a question that highlighted the concerns of so many Rhinelanders. The source of their drinking water is simulataneously the sewer for one of the world's most densely industrialized regions.

The doctor pointed out that annually over a million tons of complex, not easily decomposed, pollutants flow into the river. These include almost 4,000 tons of heavy metals and possibly forty tons of neurotoxins. With more than thirty million people relying on the river for their drinking water these were shocking statistics.

But even though he realized how corrupted it was, Doctor Starck also admitted that the river still drew him to it. It was where he chose to spend his quiet time, it was relaxing and contemplative, a place where he could reveal the secrets of growing up to his son. It was a space to forget as well as to reflect on the pressures of human development.

The tiny wooden room we were chatting in resounded with the sound of the falls. For the heart it was no matter how polluted the river was. The flow's pacifying white noise would forever draw you inwards, leading you on to the pure water world of thoughts and dreams.

Riding on past Schaffhausen along the Swiss-German border I was struck by just how quiet the setting was. Autumn colors, pastures showing the first signs of winter wheat, the smell of dung and decomposing leaves. The air was hazed with black earth, blown high from freshly tilled fields. Ancient towns dotted the riverbanks, stone hamlets unfailingly overlooked by a hilltop castle. In the wooded areas between the villages fishermen lined the shore, intently casting, reading the river and, through it, the thoughts of trout and char.

Here the Rhine may have taken on the guise of a country flow, but it was still a swift clear liquid line separating two nations: to the north German vineyards, to the south Swiss wheat and hog farms. It was hard to believe that ahead and behind were some of the heaviest concentrations of industry in the world.

It was a window onto the river at its most malleable, a silk smooth chameleon able to mutate and create within the landscape. The Rhine is a fluid impersonator who, with each turn of its banks, moves between residential, industrial and agricultural disguises. The water gives and takes and changes as seamlessly as the weather or human thought.

I was now moving into Basel, Switzerland's second largest city. It is positioned at the point were the river turns ninety degrees from a westerly direction to a straight northerly flow. This is the elbow of the Rhine. Since the time of the Romans it has been a strategically important piece of geography. Not surprisingly it was here that the first bridge spanned the river in the thirteenth century.

Today, with the cementing of Western Europe's borders, the city has become a focal point, the jewel in a wedge of land that ties together Switzerland, Germany and France. Basel is said to be the only Swiss city that doesn't look to the Alps, for it faces north towards Europe and the commercial challenges that that represents. Basel is thriving and today claims the highest per capita income of any city on the continent.

As Basel's suburbs began I kept the bike to the bank path and for the first time saw riverboats and barges using the river. The boats labored upstream and down, their diesel engines throwing out a deep-throated rumble, while rounded waves rolled away from their bows. Their decks lay close to the waterline, stacked with mountains of cargo, or covered with retractable hatches. The pilot houses were always to the rear, low flat structures that didn't offer much in the way of sight lines. From their sterns flew the flags of Switzerland, Germany, France, Holland, and Belgium. Here the river was an international highway. Basel is the beginning of the Rhine that nurtured the Industrial Revolution.

I moved into an industrial dock land. It was Saturday afternoon and surprisingly quiet, deserted but for a few ships tied up and taking on fuel or cargo. I hadn't thought that ports rested, but this was proof to the contrary.

I stopped to take some pictures and the crew of a Dutch barge invited me onboard for coffee. Their ship was spotless and I was pleasantly surprised at how well-organized the living area was, satellite TV, comfy sofas, stereo, and a well-stocked kitchen. This was the men's home away from home and they had no intentions of sacrificing their comfort.

The crew were surprised that I was not local and explained that they had assumed, because of my unshowered and disheveled appearance, that I was a resident homeless alcoholic. The sailors laughed and told me how many German alcoholics wander the country on decrepit bicycles hung with rococo arrays of bags and sacks. They are two-wheeled tramps, illiterate, Allemenian gypsies, fueled by distillates and perpetually "on the road." They frequently end up in the river cities seedy downtowns and patronize many of the same establishments as the sailors.

I enjoyed my mistaken identity and when the crew offered me a shot of rum I stayed true to my assumed identity and accepted. Soon the rum was flowing and as the afternoon wore on I asked them about life on the river. They told me how they enjoyed their work, that it was good pay, good holidays and there was the thrill of piloting a vessel along one of the most heavily trafficked stretches of water in the world. Strict regulations applied to all ships traveling the Rhine, and there was a distinct fraternity between the men, although the crew claimed, rather boozily, that, while all boatmen were brothers, they had no doubt that the Dutch boats were the best managed on the river. It was a confidence fostered by liquid courage and we all laughed at the unqualifiable nature of the statement.

I left the ship a little after sunset with a row of empty rum bottles lined up on the galley table. The crew was just getting warmed up. Ahead lay a long night in the city, but I had to find a bed so I saluted my new friends goodbye.

The next morning was Sunday and I moved north through a misty dawn as the city woke from its Sabbath slumber. Basel exuded wealth, and the area along the river was beautifully conserved. If not for the odd shred of racist graffiti adorning the stonework, I could have believed I was trapped in some theme park period piece.

The smell of fresh bread and coffee was in the air, and I saw groups of men in casual leather jackets carrying long baguettes home to their families. There was almost no traffic. The city was given over to Sunday silence and as the fog lifted to a cloudless sky an eerie calm hung over the medieval riverfront. Even the little ferry that shuttled people back and forth to the cathedral was noiseless, working its way to and fro on the silent power of the current.

I moved on into the industrial area west of the city center. This was the land of the big three, the domain of some of the world's largest drug manufacturers: Sandoz, Hoffman-LaRoche and Ciba-Geigy. Their collosal compounds were geometrical jungles of stainless steel piping, mirrored glass and colorful, strangely angled buildings. In the Sunday morning quiet they could have been mistaken for massive works of modern art. They were tributes to the corporation's power and the source of the metropolis's wealth.

However, the truth of those spotless complexes was grubbier than their appearances let on. The plants' effluents are a major cause of the Rhine's ailments. In Switzerland the allowable concentration of harmful substances disposed of in the river is six times that permitted in Germany.

The most tragic example of the environmental negligence was the toxic spill that resulted from a chemical fire in a pesticide warehouse at the Sandoz plant on November 1, 1986. In that single incident close to thirty tons of agro-chemicals, including 200 kilograms of mercury, were washed into the river as firemen doused the blaze.

As a result, 300 kilometers of the Rhine suffered serious ecological damage; over half a million fish were killed, including the Rhine's entire eel population. The irony of the catastrophe was that the different governments had just held a meeting to congratulate each other for a decade of intense conservation on the river.

I crossed into France past a group of unquestioning, cigarette smoking guards in a tin shack border post. The concentration of industry continued into Saint Louis, the French extension of Basel, but after a few kilometers the industrial parks petered out and I left the city.

I was following the Rhine, but the river had changed. Once it entered France the flow was channeled into a gargantuan, concrete banked canal and forced in an inorganically straight line to the north. The

Rhine had been imprisoned and in the process had lost its character. The solid, algae-stained, cement banks were splashed by oddly symetrical waves, the result of the unending line of riverboats that charged back and forth. From the spry Arcadian flow of a hundred kilometers before, the Rhine had been transformed into a liquid robot that moved under the spell of some mathematically inclined master.

North from Basel the Rhine moves through a wide plain bordered on one flank by the heights of the Schwarzwald and on the other by the Vosges Hills. Until the beginning of the last century, the river through this area was three to four kilometers wide and moved languorously between those hilly boundaries. Geographically there was little to oppose its movement, and the plain became a wide expanse of marshland meadows too saturated for agricultural use. In the dampness of the valley bottom typhoid, dysentery and the feared bog fever were rampant. For the new school of business-minded burghers it was a disgrace to waste such potentially productive land.

In 1812 an army officer and engineer named Gottfried Tulla proposed an extensive reformation of the Rhine's course. The local populace, with a Luddite fear of disturbing old father Rhine, gathered opposition and the work at times had to be undertaken with the aid of military guardianship. However, by 1876 the project had been completed, and the upper Rhine was straightened and consequently shortened by eighty-two kilometers. The expansive river had been compressed into a 200-meter-wide channel, 10,000 hectares of fertile soils had been cajoled from the wetlands, and the engineers hailed it as a triumph of man over nature.

The local population, after appreciating that their opposition would be unheeded, accepted the new Rhine, but over time they inherited something even more exasperating than mosquitoes and diarrhea — the lowering of their groundwater table. The problem has plagued the area to this day. Soil dehydration, because of the increased draw of the faster flowing river, has resulted in water shortage problems throughout one of

Germany's most agriculturally productive regions. Wells have to be dug deeper and deeper and water conservation measures, costing billions of dollars, have been implemented, all at the expense of the farmers that the grand project was supposed to assist.

Dehydration was one concern, but the engineers had also increased the river's capability to carry silt and sand, 1,000 cubic meters a day, and with this material new islands and sandbars emerged. The dream of the businessmen, regular large scale shipping, was extinguished, and the life of the small, independent river bargers continued.

But the French government's desire to use the Rhine for commercial shipping was solved with the building of La Grand Canal d'Alsace, the newer waterway that runs north from Basel. The canal utilizes seven barrages to funnel the current through possible areas of silt congestion, and ten locks to raise and lower traffic around a controversial set of hydroelectric plants.

The French gained the right to use the river for energy after the post-World War One Treaty of Versailles, and the first station at Kembs was completed in 1932. Today the Kembs locks service more than eighty boats a day, and the system of dams produces 13 percent of France's hydropower. The canal, the dams and the locks are all pieces of national pride for the French, for the right to construct them was paid for with the lives of those lost in the bloodied mud of the Somme and Verdun. They are a finger in the face of their Teutonic neighbor.

I stood at Kembs and watched as the basin filled with water and raised a pair of Dutch barges to the river's upper level. It was humbling to see. The water surged violently in through the lock's rear doors and elevated the two boats like ducks in a rusty bathtub. A small crowd had gathered to watch the show, an afternoon family outing.

It is difficult not be awed by the canal, where at some points the water level can be ten meters above the road that parallels it to the west. It is a surreal sensation to watch the smoke stacks of ships float by above you. All that day I pedaled on reclaimed land along a road aptly named "le Route d'Electricitè de France." There were no houses for five hundred meters from the water and the fields that took up the space were freshly tilled in anticipation of a winter crop. It was a planar landscape, a piece of earth that until 150 years ago did not exist.

The next morning I woke to the sound, for the first time in three weeks, of rain against my tent roof. I packed in a light drizzle and pushed my heavily weighted cycle out to the road in a thick fog. The woods around me resembled the forests of some misty fairytale world.

I rode again in the shadow of the canal bank. With the deep hum of marine diesels above me and the mist entering every available cleft in my clothing I felt like an aquatic being, moving sluggishly below the waterline.

The fog itself was so dense that on the heavily trafficked road I was scared. Trucks emerged out of the netherworld, their air horns blaring and trouble lights flashing. The juggernauts pushed me off the slick asphalt only to suck me right back into their soaking wake. I could feel the drivers, as they saw my tiny sodden figure, grip tighter to their steering wheels and swear at me in gutter French.

By 11 a.m. the fog was lifting and I came to Marckolsheim, a small quiet village built on a nondescript piece of the Alsatian plain. But Marckolsheim's place in history is insured by an overgrown concrete bunker on its outskirts, a monument to the Maginot Line.

La Ligne Maginot was the heavily fortified French defensive position that stretched along the Rhine from the Alps to the border with Luxembourg. Constructed in the 1930s as a deterrent to Hitler's Lebensraum desires, it became a monolithic red herring for a France that was fighting the twin evils of a depressed economy and an aggressive neighbor.

The Line was the keystone in France's interwar security policy, but when the hammer came down in 1939, the German Wehrmacht easily circumvented it through lightly defended Luxembourg. The impassable Maginot Line had become a sour joke. The scores of interconnected fortresses and bunkers, designed on the lessons learned from the devastation of the Great War, were ineffectual in the Blitzkrieg (lightning war) that saw Hitler take Paris in ten days.

It was unnerving to walk around the deserted site. The mist still hung in the trees and, since it was not tourist season, I was alone with a huge, silent dune of concrete named Casemate 53-3. An unearthly quiet surrounded the park, no wind, no sound of far-off traffic. Massive bomb craters, pooled with stagnant water, spoke of the 50-year-old aerial attacks by screaming Stuka dive bombers, and the twisted metal and exposed rebar were evidence of the deadly spray of artillery and heavy machine gun fire.

It was a relic, a solid memory from an era of hatred and distrust, a time when the Rhine was a border between good and evil, an entity to be cherished by one nation over another. The bunker housed the ghosts of that generation, the ghosts of men who had died for their country without having been given the chance to fight. Marckolsheim could have been a peaceful place to die, but the Maginot Line, with its hundreds of kilometers of confrontational concrete and steel, destroyed that fantasy.

The next day the low clouds still clung to the earth. Now I was riding through the industrial region south of Strasbourg. I passed an area filled with recycling plants. Lining the road, mountains of subtly sweet-smelling compost steamed in the cool air, the peaks of the manure obscured by mist.

I crossed a bridge and looked down to see, in a man-made pool below me, a brigade of military engineers in the throes of building a temporary bridge parallel to the one I was on. In the mist-mired, half-speed reality that I had been riding in it was a scene of intense action. Halos of orange light from banks of sodium floodlights floated in the fog. The pond shrieked with the sound of cutting metal and showers of sparks from a squad of acetylene torches danced on the water. Loud speakers hailed the morning orders and khaki bodies in fluorescent flak vests bustled in and out of the shrouded shadows. It could have been a scene from Vimy Ridge, or the Ardennes or Dien Bien Phu, military zeal in a steaming dreamscape, and I thought perhaps that is the way soldiers have to make their way through a war zone, with the help of half-vision.

I moved out of the Dante-esque vignette, and as I came down off the span I saw three municipal workers, impervious to the feverish simultaneous building going on a hundred meters away, welding the underbelly of the real life bridge. Same work, separate realities.

I moved through the industrial fringe of the city, a zone where old and new collide, the massive container warehouses and holding pens of the multinational transport concerns bordered the brick shipping yards of centuries-old barge companies. The river has been displaced by the road, as the transit zones of society's raw materials have shifted inland. Wooden-tabled eateries and zinc-shelved wine bars have given way to the concrete encased, transcontinental truck stop — restaurant, gas station, bar, motel, and heavy equipment garage all in one. From the edge of Strasbourg I saw that modernization is miniaturization.

But a wrong turn in the matrix of the truck stops brought me onto the main thoroughfare north into the city. Suddenly I was surrounded by 18-wheeled transports and, to avoid getting swamped, was pedaling like a man possessed. My back was running with sweat and the truckers all honked their horns — whether in delight at seeing a human scurrying like a scared rabbit or because I was moving at a Tour de France pace I couldn't be sure. I saw a pullout off to my left and, panting hard, swung my bike onto a one-lane bridge, feeling like I'd just pulled out of the running of the bulls in Pamplona.

I followed the road, and as I moved towards the city center the buildings lining the streets became older and closed in tight around the traffic. Soon I found myself in the midst of a web of one-way streets, surrounded by boulangeries, patesseries and the smell of morning bread. It was a pedestrian zone and I pushed my bike through a maze of cobbled lanes that led to the Strasbourg's hub, the cathedral.

In the cathedral square the church appeared in all its Gothic glory. The building was, in its day, the tallest in all Christendom, a gargantuan filigreed fantasy, a medieval play on space, mass and light. I was humbled by its detail and scale, and, for a second, sensed exactly what a fifteenth-century peasant must have felt upon seeing the monolith for the first time — intimidation and wonderment. The cathederal was the medieval architectural interpretation of God.

My North American eyes are adjusted to the lines of modernity: simple, clear-cut slices in architectural space — functional and neat. But here was a building that had so many nonapplicable appendages that it had more connection to South Indian Hindu temples than to the geometric spires of the world's new economic religions. I tried to appreciate it for what it was, enamored by the vision and craftsmanship of the builders, but it was too massive, or perhaps I was in too big a rush, and I left feeling like I had forgotten something.

I had lunch by the statue of Marshall Leclerc, Strasbourg's liberator from the Nazis. His shoulders were a pigeon perch splattered with avian effluent, and his metallic head, green with age, looked to the heavens. But the general is only the latest in a long line of emancipators because, with its strategic positioning on the Rhine, Strasbourg has been the most fought over city in Europe.

The Romans inhabited the original Celtic townsite, but in the fifth century it gave way to "barbarians" from across the Rhine. By 842 the Strasbourg covenant was sealed, the first text to be written in both Romanesque and Tudesque (Germanic) languages. As Germany and France gathered influence and identity, Strasbourg became the pawn in their continental chess game, a coveted symbol that defined which of the two was stronger at any given time.

In the Thirty Years War (1616-48) the city was neutral, but after the Treaties of Westphalia it inherited a weak position and was pressured to submit to the armies of Louis XIV. Strasbourg moved from being a free city of the German empire to a French royal town. It struggled through the French Revolution and the Napoleonic empire, but was claimed again by the Germans during the Franco-Prussian War in 1870, when it became the capital for the provinces of Alsace-Lorraine. In 1918, yet again, the town reverted to French rule, but in 1939 became a Germanic province. Finally on November 23, 1944, the 2nd Armored Division under Leclerc freed the city from its most recent occupation.

Appropriately in 1949 it was made the "Capital of Europe." The home first to the Council of Europe and later to the European Parliament, the city has, through all its incarnations, stayed true to its name, Strasbourg, "city at the crossroads."

On the way out of town that afternoon I was passed by a black man, wearing a black jacket, riding a black bicycle. He went by in a flash, his bike squealing from its thirst for oil, and his rear tire so warped it gave the cycle the jerky motion of a circus vehicle. He slowed and I caught up to him. We exchanged "bonjours" and rode side by side for a while. Jean-Louis spoke heavily accented English and we talked about how, along with his family, he had come as a child from Cameroon.

I asked him how he liked France. He replied, "OK yeh, but I like America more." It turned out that Jean-Louis had never visited America. I asked what he thought about the Rhine, the river that he had lived by for the past decade. He said that although it wasn't so important to him it was integral to France: "After all it is our border with Germany."

Jean-Louis' statement was notable. In France I got the sense that the river was the definitive piece of borderline geography. In Germany it is part of the national psyche. In both cases it is considered elemental to the country — it is the ultimate symbol of riverborne nationalism. The idea has haunted the Rhine since the first days of human occupation. It is a boundary between us and them. This feeling probably reached its peak in the nineteenth century with the shifting back and forth of not only Strasbourg, but the river that fostered the city.

The poet and nationalist Ernst Mortiz Arndt, summed up Germany's nineteenth-century feeling best when he wrote, "Der Rhine — Teutschlands Strom, aber nicht Teutschlands Gränze" (The Rhine — Germany's river but not Germany's boundary). Yet, only a few years before that in 1792, the Lord Mayor of Strasbourg, Baron de Dietrich, sang for the first time the *Chant de guerre de l'Armèe du Rhin* (War song of the Rhine army) — the song that would become, under the title the *Marseillaise*, the French national anthem.

The river shifted between nations as simply as the cartographers could move the red line on their maps. Heinrich Heine, the German poet, retaliated against the literary nationalists and added another layer to the possessive confusion by stating that the only people justified to lay any claim to the Rhine were the Rheinlanders themselves. Yet in all this tribalistic mayhem possibly the feelings of the river are summed up best in the words of Father Rhine himself from Scheffel's poem, *Der Tompeter von Säckingen*:

> And through the sand
> which fills me with such deadly hate
> I drag my tired existence
> And I died long before
> The sea, my grave, enfolds me.

The next day the fog gave way to rain, the mist had turned solid and those solids, drawn by gravity, fell to earth. In an autumn oak forest I packed my sodden camp and headed north again in a blizzard of golden leaves. The shimmering wet pavement sizzled like bacon beneath my wheels. The trucks that passed me pushed up leafy yellow and rust tornadoes that danced around me as if happy to be airborne. Fall was turning to winter and the change was ushered in with color and movement.

127

I passed through small French villages, the bedroom communities of Strasbourg. They weren't really quaint, just plain sets of brick houses, trimmed with commuter cars in concrete-lined driveways and flowerbeds out of bloom. As the German border neared, I ventured back to the river and found that the last sight the Rhine beholds before leaving France is a derelict port, an assembly of rusty derricks and rickety landings. Fitting, I thought — of all the nations it flowed through, France, with its barrages, dams, atomic energy plants and mountains of gravel, cherished the river the least.

I crossed another nonexistent border into Germany and the Bienwald forest. The highway was bordered with uncannily symmetrical lines of trees. Rows of similar species led out from the road in such straight lines that it made it hard to call it a forest. To my east was Karlsruhe, the first of the many industrial towns the river passes through on its path through Germany. I was entering the German heartland, the region where so much of the nation's history has been written. Western Germany's past is a narrative that winds around the river.

I pushed on. The forest opened out onto gray farmland. Tractors adorned every field and each village that I found, tucked behind hillocks, was a self-contained unit, little outposts in the web of urbanity that had grown up along the river.

Even though only the hundred meters of the river separated them, Germany felt different than France. It was hard to pinpoint the root of the feeling. Maybe it was the insinuated structure of the towns or the air of subconscious but always implied efficiency.

The back roads returned me to the river and I found myself in Speyer, one of the great imperial cities of the ancient Rheinland Palatinate. Like so many of its contemporaries the town is dominated by its cathedral. I rode around it, marveling again at the scale that the ancient aristocracy believed was needed to appease God, and then made my way to the museum shop to have a cup of coffee.

I was soaked, a wet rat, with lank hair and mud-spattered rain pants. A voice asked me in English if I was from Speyer, and I replied with a sheepish, "No," wondering if again I was about to be confused for the local drunk.

The questioner was the clerk, a large man with a well-groomed beard and button-down shirt. "I didn't think so," he said. "I'm American. Let me buy you another coffee."

He had the look and demeanor of a college Christian but turned out to be married to a German and harbored no missionary urges. Over our drinks he told me a little of the cathedral's story, and in that context it made some sense that a foreigner would be working there, at a church whose tumultuous past echoes the history of the whole of northeastern Europe.

The foundation stones for Speyer Cathedral were laid by the Salian king, Conrad II, in 1030, and the original construction was completed sometime around 1100. It continued to be added onto by subsequent dynasties until the fifteenth century. Then, in 1689, during the Palatinate succession war, it was destroyed and not completely rebuilt until 1778, but was again devastated in 1795 in the campaigns following the French Revolution, only to be yet again resurrected in 1817. The cathedral survived the bombing raids of 1944 to '45 relatively unscathed, but was, between 1957 and '66, completely restored in an attempt to recover the original Salian architecture.

In the multitude of styles that had been layered upon the original, the core of the structure had been lost. What was intended to be the seminal cathedral had become a wedding cake of history, layer upon layer of dynasties and empires piled one on top of the other. It was the object for countless benefactors to throw money at and, in some way, gain a piece of immortality. As King Ludwig I of Bavaria, one of its many patrons, noted, the purpose of philanthropy was to "increase the glory of God, the triumph of the arts and his [the king's] own posthumous fame through a new creation."

Speyer Cathedral was the largest building of its age and became the mother church for a diocese that spread far on both sides of the

Rhine. During the Middle Ages it was renowned around the Christian world for its miracle-working image of the Madonna, and Speyer became a place of pilgrimage, a situation promoted by its proximity to the river. The pilgrims brought with them not only piety but also ideas and business that enhanced the wealth and prestige of the city. Fifty times the Holy Roman Empire's Imperial Diet met within the cathedral's confines, and in its crypt, eight emperors, three empresses and two imperial chancellors are buried.

But possibly the act that Speyer and its cathedral will be remembered for far into the future is the Imperial Council meeting of 1529, which decided that the rights of the area's newly evolved Lutheran citizens were to be annulled. The representatives of the new order left the cathedral and from that day on their denomination became known as the "Protestants." The clerk at the museum shop summed it up, "The survival of this place is a set of small miracles. You know, even though the river lies only a few hundred meters away, there has never been, in the cathedral's 950-year history, a recorded instance of the church being flooded. It's a miracle," and then he added with a wry smile, "to those looking for them."

I stayed at the youth hostel that night in a room populated by new pilgrims. My roommates were all workers at the airplane factory near the river. Mark, a Briton, Arif, an Iranian, and Franz, an East German from Saxony, were all to some extent "Auslander arbeiters," foreign workers. They were there for the money, and the tight rental market in Speyer forced them to lodge at the hostel. Over dinner they asked me my business, and when I told them that I was interested in the river they grew animated and each of them told me about their own rivers.

Franz told of childhood memories by the Elbe near Dresden. Arif spoke about the importance of water in his desert home near Isfahan, and Mark talked about how, in the summer, he would sit by the banks of the Rhine late in the evening and watch the barges and tugs maneuvering expertly from shore to shore through mobs of chaotic marine traffic.

They all cherished those memories of their particular watercourse — they had all dreamt of the river. It was universal — three countries and three different visions of childhood, industry, and survival. The river was the ultimate conversation piece, a line of everflowing thought that meandered quietly into the darkest recesses of the mass unconscious.

I moved on up the river to Ludwigshafen and Mannheim. Mannheim, the second largest river port in Germany, is on the Rhine's eastern shore and directly opposite it lies the larger-than-life Ludwigshafen BASF factory.

The Baderisch Anilin and Soda Fabrik (BASF) complex was a prototype for the industrial comglomerates that have come to dominate the Western world. Inside a razor wire fenced compound that spreads for kilometers BASF manufactures everything from fertilizer to vitamins and employs upwards of 40,000 people.

The company was founded in 1865 when an efficient method of utilizing anilines, an indispensable element in the manufacture of dyes, plastics and explosives, was discovered. With that one landmark innovation an industrial dynasty was built. Ludwigshafen and Mannheim developed as a base for the fledgling industry — they were new towns ripe for new industries. The older cities, such as Speyer and Worms, were left to their history, too old to catch the next wave of development.

Business is mobile, able to transcend man-made boundaries, but in order to survive it needs markets and transportation. The Rhine provides both. The river has attracted agricultural settlers since before the time of the Romans, and has been a ready corridor between the clustered towns and cities that evolved. Steam, the great energy innovation of the nineteenth century, solidified those links by providing the transportation consistency that business needed to fully utilize the river.

It took me twenty minutes to ride the length of the BASF complex with its concrete and steel office towers standing alongside steaming refinery chimneys. The entire apparatus of a multinational matrix lay there behind the barbed wire. That single compound was an economic power that touched every corner of the globe. It was strange to think that so much of what we want and strive for, the carrots of our existence, wants as well as products, were generated from within the walls of one single organization.

I rode back to the Rhine and looked across at Mannheim. The river was abuzz with tugs, pushing and pulling great squared-off lighters filled with granulates and ores and tarpaulined loads. The tugs moved as watery sheepdogs, hustling to and fro around the scows, front and back, nudging them first one way and then another, positioning the barges correctly so as to load or unload. The roar of engines moved up and down through the scales, a euphonic accompaniment to the work.

In the background slate gray hills made of scrap steel and rusting piles of iron lay in an undulating wasteland of the used and reused. Above them five massive cranes swiveled, geometric ostriches, weaving back and forth on separate sets of tracks, screeching as metal stroked metal, their individual paths interconnecting from my far-off view. They swung gracefully in one direction, swooping and scooping with long triangulated arms, grasping up bursting loads of jagged steel, and then unceremoniously dumping them in some other predetermined location.

Shuffling into the foreground of this grunge ballet of water and industry came an old man on crutches, trailed by an equally aged dog dragging a limp leash. The man wore a leather driving coat and black polyester slacks, and his tweed cap was pulled low over his eyes. His dog, a long-haired German shepherd well into its waning years, looked up indifferently as his master caught sight of me.

The old man straightened his back and asked in German if I was on a bike tour. I replied in the positive and, with the silent encouragement of the old and lonely, told him of my plans. He nodded his head, not so energetically, and asked, sweeping his hand out at the activity on the water, what I thought of "Germany's great river." I replied that there was some awkward beauty to the movement going on. He nodded again, this time with his head bowed, and said, "Yes, I don't know if I would call it beauty, but it got us back our country. That river helped us, maybe inspired us to pull ourselves back from the destruction of the war."

It was a powerful thought — Germany demoralized after yet another drawn out and humiliating defeat, looking for inspiration, ploughing its past for images of a greater time, needing a vision so all encompassing that an entire nation could fall back on it. The river, with its legends and history, its lineage of greatness through the good times and the bad, was just such a symbol.

For the old man, it was a place to retire to when history became too overwhelming. By the river he could rest in the arms of a glorious past and remind himself how he had helped resurrect a legend. We chatted a while longer and then he politely excused himself, saying his dog was anxious to continue their walk. They moved away, a past full of memories. They were a slow motion pas de deux set against the Rhine's unending jazz swing.

Out of Ludwigshafen I pedaled back into farmland. Here the soil was different than in the Alsace, a finer texture, a sandier loam. The air was again gray from the newly tilled fields. Tractors shuffled, like an army of landlocked crustaceans, across endless stretches of chestnut earth, ploughing, planting, picking, digging. But I never saw people in those fields, the new farmers were all ensconced in red or green four-wheel-drive tractors.

Ten kilometers farther on and again I found myself in one of the old imperial cities, Worms, another piece of history embodied by a set of churches and graveyards.

I arrived at the cathedral as the nuns let out their kindergarten class, and a frenzy of squeals and waving of hands accompanied the onset of freedom. The children dispersed in a dying wave of sound and the nuns got into a suspiciously sporty Audi sedan and pulled out of the church parking lot in a rush of gravel.

The cathedral was so collared by buildings and trees that the huge structure appeared cramped, its flying buttresses pushed out into not quite enough space. History, I realized, can distend architecture. Chronological space with such buildings can encroach upon the physical. I've visited small caves in the Himalayas, the homes of great meditators, that felt huge. The cathedral was such a place, large to start with but made larger by its personal narrative. It was now something beyond the boundaries of what its builders had originally envisioned.

The original cathedral was a product of the Romanesque boom of the eleventh and twelfth centuries, but was constructed on a base formed by a Roman coliseum from the time just after Christ when the town was known as Civitas Vangionum. For the Burgundians of the third century it was a capital, and under Charlemagne it was the site of one of the emperor's favorite residences. During the time of the Holy Roman Empire it was where the first imperial tax, the "Germeiner Pfennig," was introduced.

But, as with Speyer, its place in history is guaranteed by its connection to Protestantism. It was here in 1521 that Martin Luther was called before Emperor Charles V and asked to retract his "insane doctrines." Luther refused, believing that this was opposed to his conscience with God. With this one act the schism within the church commenced, and the age of the individually responsible Christian was initiated.

The next morning I went to see the Holy Sand, the largest Jewish cemetery in Europe. Within a stone's throw of the cathedral, the cemetery and a synagogue are all that remain of what was once one of the most important Jewish communities on the continent.

The cemetery sits behind a high stone wall, its one entrance leading in past an old house. As I entered the caretakers cutting the lawns looked on nonchalantly. In the early light the field was a patchwork of green and gold, freshly cut grass, lichen-covered headstones, sun streaks breaking through the clouds, and maple leaves the color of turmeric lying at odd angles to the graves. The traffic noise was silenced by the wall, and in the little sanctuary all was peaceful; history was silent. There were lives in those stones, granite blocks chiseled in indecipherable Yiddish, twisted and turned like the tortured people they represented, angled like uncertain mountains. It was a magic moment, as light and shadow played for me, and I sank onto the dew-wet grass to let the past seep in.

Lying down I couldn't help but think about the cultures that the river had brought into its midst — Romans and Jews from the south, Vikings and Gauls from the north. The graveyard was a piece of that history but the river was the avenue along which those stories moved.

I made my way slowly out of Worms and cut a line to the northwest that pulled me away from the river and overland directly for Bingen. This was some of the most productive wine country in Germany, and I wanted to see the region that produces the ambrosia that has become so closely associated with the river.

The earth rose in a set of rolling hills. I climbed and climbed and found myself surrounded by ridges of red-brown earth planted with row after infinite row of trellised grape vines. This was the home of Bacchus, the land of his perpetual pleasure. The queues of dormant vines lent a strange alignment to the landscape, as precisely paralleled tiers of withered, hibernating shrubs angled south, facing the sun, an accentuating, linear overlay to the landscape's feminine curves. The last russet leaves and the odd bunch of ice wine grapes still clung to the branches, waiting for the first frosts. It was a land moving into the season of rest.

In the bright, obtuse, early winter light the fields were barren and no people walked the rows of sleeping vines. In this season the land was a Bacchanalian wilderness. Above me thick cloud banks moved north to meet the hills and the wind came hard from the west, beating me, calling me to put my back into the pedals and fight for those kilometers away from the river.

I passed villages, each one situated in a hollow, a sunlit vale out of the wind. I would roll down into the town letting gravity pull me and would then have to push hard, fighting the uphill grind on the way out. The air in the valleys was tinged with the smell of fermentation, tangy and slightly sour, different than on the hills where the wind rolled by, pulling with it the resinous scent of distant forests. Above one village a wind power station whirred, the mighty blades of the generators making thick whooshing noises with each pass by my head.

In every community "weinguts" proliferated, the crests of the different wine houses set into their walls framed within antique casks. The cellars were of stone, polished cobbled floors, clean and efficient, and the courtyards bustled with luxury cars and heavy machinery.

From Genslingen I could see the course of the river just beyond Bingen, working its way patiently west along the southern edge of the Taunus range, looking for the opening, the Bingen Hole, the breach that would draw it north to Westphalia.

I dropped into a long, gently sloping downhill, and tucked myself into the handlebars to relish the most speed I'd felt since the Alps. Houses, people, roadsigns and barking dogs all rushed by. Children waved and shouted from fields and roadsides. I was watching a hundred lives flash before my eyes — it was as if, for a second, I was the river, and the lives of those on the banks were subtly touched by my presence.

Bingen is a strange place, a tourist resort, an Atlantic City on the Rhine with discos by the water and sleek long-hulled riverboats tied up on its docks. Bands of tourists, wrapped for winter, wandered the streets perusing cheap emporiums selling kitschy Rhine paraphernalia and boutiques with the latest imitations of Milanese fashion.

But the town is also famous as the home of the mystic saint, Hildegard of Bingen, who in the twelfth century electrified the Christian world with her spiritual compositions and visionary theological scripts. With her writing of *Scivias*, (*Know the Ways*) Hildegard earned the title Prophetissa Teutonica and with her further commentaries, *Liber Vitae Meritorium* and *Liber Diviorum*, she became, along with Bernard of Clairvaux, the occident's acknowledged spiritual authority.

In commemoration of her 900th birth anniversary there were numerous celebrations planned in Bingen. Strangely, many of them offered tutelage in the different schools of new spirituality — the deep contemplation of a visionary had been given over to New Age fusion. Bingen, with its clairvoyant nuns and raves on the Rhine, was itself a hybrid, evidence of a people searching for soulful inspiration.

At Bingen the Nahe River enters the Rhine from the south and the enlarged flow cuts hard north into the Taunus Hills through the Bingen Hole. Interesting, I thought, that Hildegard would choose this point where the river moves into the land, an inverse Haridwar, as the site of her visions.

The watercourse's first architectural greeting on its passage through the gorge is the Mäuseturm, the Mouse Tower, the first of a series of historical toll posts through this riverine bottleneck. Despite the Saxon legend that Archbishop Hatto I was nibbled to death by mice, the origin of the tower's name lies not with the rodents but with the "maut," the customs duty traditionally levied on all traffic. The slit windows and imposing height of the structure recalled a time when the tariff was taken by force if necessary.

Off to the east, on the horizon above the town of Rudesheim I could make out the colossal Germania statue, a 12-meter female representation of German nationalism. In her right hand she holds the imperial crown, the proof of her regency and in her left a sword, the instrument of its insurance. She has stood there at the entrance to the Rhine's strategic narrows since 1883 when, on the orders of Kaiser Wilhelm, scores of Prussian cannons were melted down for her casting.

Forged from the iron of German nationalism she stares unwaveringly southwest, to the land of historic opposition, France, the nation that those same cannons had defeated a dozen years before. One hundred and ten years on, in an era of globalization, it would be simplistic to say that German nationalism is a dying cause, because each year over two million tourists still make the pilgrimage to stand at her feet.

The Bingen Hole marks the start of the section of the river that, through picture books and secondhand legends, is known the world over as "the romantic Rhine." The modern mythology of the gorge is a product of the early ninteenth century English Romantics, who were a byproduct of accelerating industrial development and a desire to hold onto a sentimental history.

After the openness of the wine lands the gorge felt tight. The hills rose sharply on either side and, with the light falling behind the ridge to the south, the place took on a cool glow. There was a tangible romance to the scene. When the shady slopes were struck by slashes of golden dusk, and the hills, thick with crumbling castles and wintering vineyards, trapped the gorge's silver-lined mists, it was not hard to believe that this was the home of princesses and knights on white horses. But there was a reality to the dream that was impossible to ignore. The blatant truth was traffic.

The gorge has historically been the simplest way to move from south to north in the most densely populated region of Germany. Both sides of the river are taken up by roads and rail tracks — 18,000 vehicles and 350 trains roar by each day. On the river navigational buoys sway in the hard current, and the barges, tugs, riverboats, and lighters lumbering up and down the canyon outnumber the trains. With trains whistling, cars rushing by with heedless speed, and the riverboats blowing clouds of diesel to shore, the valley is a long way from the silent, contemplative romance of Shelley, Byron and Turner.

By 5 p.m. the canyon was dark and I had reached Bacharach. It is a conservator's dream village, with delicate shops set into a street that looks as though it had deviated little in the past three hundred years. But it was too clean, too preserved, and I had to wonder if the American composer and singer Burt Bacharach, himself a living example of kitsch, had decided upon his own name after visiting the village.

I climbed away from the river towards the hostel that loomed above the community like some evil fortress. It was a mighty climb and by the time I reached the Stahleck castle and staggered past the portcullis I was drenched in sweat and beyond breath.

But the ascent was worth it. The view was fantastic and the citadel had been positioned, in the tradition of the toll collection strongholds, so as to provide the greatest possible view of the river. I stood in the main courtyard as the sun lowered itself to the Taunus Hills, and could see barges as far away as Lorch winding their way north on a thread of golden water. As I watched the sky turned a salmon pink and almost instantaneously the cars and trains bustling through the gorge clicked on their headlights. I saw an army of speeding ants emerging out of blackness, while the sky moved towards the color of the earth.

The spell was broken by the shrieks of a horde of school children who came running en masse at the low castle wall that guarded a fifty-meter drop to a stony field. I was surrounded by a gang of effervescent dwarfs, the boys threatening to toss the girls from the battlements and the girls in turn screaming in mock horror. The romance of the Rhine was being played out in hyper-reality. I was trapped in the castle of the high school gnomes. The kids were contemporary princes and princesses, acting out the legends in Chicago Bulls caps and Levi jeans.

My room was a surprise: clean, warm and with a view of the river. My only roommate was a college hockey player called Pat who was traveling for the first time. I asked him the usual questions about the Rhine and he waxed eloquently about the river he had traveled along that day from Cologne.

"Man, it's wicked you know, I think it's so cool, just the way everything is so old, you can really feel the history, everything's half ruined. I mean, shit, it's the first time I've seen any castles and I'm staying in one . . . Now that's cool." For him Germany was the Munich Oktoberfest and anything he saw of the country beyond that was cream. Bacharach had pushed Pat's vocabulary of superlatives to the extreme.

Old is gold when it is associated with the Rhine, tourist gold anyway. The river was one of the first areas to attract mass tourism. After the late eighteenth- and early nineteenth-century French revolutionary wars, and the abatement of Napoleon's continental blockade in 1814, the area began to actively pursue tourist business. The region was especially attractive to young English travelers for whom the Rhine, with its Gothic-Romantic ambience, was the height of nineteenth-century adventure tourism.

With the advent of cross-channel steamboats and the opening of the railway in 1844, the gorge area was only a single day's journey from London and tourism became a possibility for the emerging middle classes. The rush was on, and the Rhine valley has never looked back. The tourists still flock to it, but with time and changing fortunes it has managed to lure people from far beyond the continent. The English still come, but now primarily in caravan trailers or on Eurail passes. The North Americans perpetuated the rush with a new wave of romance seekers in the 1960s and '70s. Today the slack has been absorbed by the Asians, to whom the Rhine is as exotic today as it was to those first travelers almost two hundred years ago.

I continued north and, near Kaub, came across the monument that marks the point where, on New Year's Eve 1813, Prinz Blücher von Wahlstadt forded the river. His crossing, immortalized in poetry and art, is a point of memorization for German schoolchildren, as it marks a high point in the perpetual struggle between Europe's two continental superpowers.

Between 1801-06 the Rhineland states seceded from the German Reich and with that the Holy Roman Empire of German Nations, an institution that had somehow survived six hundred tumultuous years, imploded. In its wake the already tenuous union of princely states and free cities disintegrated. Many of the principalities in the western part of the empire aligned themselves with the harbinger of this chaos, Napoleon, while in the east Prussia survived to literally fight another day.

With their victory over Napoleon in the Battle of Leipzig in 1813 the Rhenish states returned to the German fold and Blücher, chasing the retreating French forces, crossed and thus secured "Germany's river" on that freezing New Year's night. The map of Europe was restructured a year later at the Congress of Vienna, and the entity that evolved from the Prussian victories formed the basis of what we now know as Germany.

On the "French" side of the river the monument is a simple marble plaque immortalizing Blücher. There, surrounded by motorways, high speed trains and manufactured history, the notion that there was a time when a united Germany was only a dream seemed far away. Cars rushed by, riverboats moved back and forth, and the Rhine flowed ceaselessly onwards. I thought of how history, like the river, is movement, and the words that record it are merely the driftwood that is washed to shore, random shards of time, to be connected by those lucky enough to retrieve them.

I had been keeping my eyes on the kilometer markers along the river, waiting for number 544 — the spot that marks the Lorelei. The Lorelei was immortalized by the poem of Clemens Brentano, who, working with the area's ancient folklore, envisioned a siren temptress residing on the hilltop. She is a Teutonic Medusa, enticing lovelorn sailors in the direction of her rocky lair, causing the sinking of many a ship. She is, of course, depicted as a blonde maiden, naked but for the smile that adorns her beautiful face.

It was a vision that appealed to the mid-twentieth-century National Socialist, Aryan mythology. Interestingly, the contemporary songs in her honor by the Jewish poet Heinrich Heine were so popular that it was impossible for the Nazis to quash his work. They settled by letting the masses sing a song whose composer was unmentionable. Perhaps, for those years, the memory of Heine was absorbed by the same spirit who had snatched the souls from the multitude of sailors.

At kilometer 544 I had expected more, for after all it was the scene of a song that had tugged at the hearts of an entire nation for 150 years. Possibly it was the commercialization of the area, right down to tours of the fictional nymph's village house and the Lorelei café with its overpriced coffee. No doubt the wet whir of the constant traffic played havoc with the imagery. But the crux was the busload of Japanese tourists, all in neon colored rain jackets and immaculate shoes, snapping pictures of the cliff and singing in unison a heavily accented version of Heine's anthem. The myth was an international phenomenon and mine must have been a selfish vision of the naked nymph.

Small towns kept rolling by — Boppard with its vineyards, Filsen with its view to the north and south, and Spay with its allegiances to commercial shipping. Soon I was moving into Koblenz, caught in the traffic, dragged along like a piece of scrap paper. The flow of vehicles pulled me to the point from which the city draws its name, in Latin "Confluentes," the confluence of the Rhine and its most important tributary, the Mosel. It is the point known as Deutsches Eck, Germany's Neck. This is the connecting point between the nation's heart, the Rhine, and its belly, the Mosel.

There I was greeted by Kaiser Wilhelm I, a metaled and massive mustachioed statue that stands upon a pedestal the size of a palace. He is green and gargantuan, an historical Incredible Hulk, astride a panting stallion, his face adorned with its ubiquitous facial hair, blowing in the winds of time. He is serious and focused. Kaiser Wilhelm was a man with a job to do and his work was nation building. He is the monarch who resurrected the German state, rebuilt the glory of the Reich, and with the masterful help of his right hand man, Bismarck, united the Germany that we now accept as timeless. His likeness fittingly dominates the scene at the meeting of these two most German of rivers.

The site was throbbing with indigenous tourists, the bus people, streaming from their chrome coaches, clutching SLRs and patent leather handbags, the guides herding them to the feet of the emperor and pointing purposefully to the father of the Fatherland. The whole scene touched me eerily, for it was resurgent Germania, the pull of power. The utter immensity of the statue was disconcerting. It was an image that had been torn down in 1945 as a bad memory of the Nazi days and then revived in 1993. Rust never sleeps.

I left as another wave of tourists was disgorged from their bus and stood gaping at the monstrosity. In the base of the statue two children were playing, shouting out commands and giving each other salutes like Kaisers or Fuhrers. There was laughing all around, but the question lingered for me, how real was it all?

I followed the Mosel into the city in search of the Middle Rhine Museum and was happy to find, inside a beautiful pastel building set back into a cobbled square, a simple collection of romantic paintings depicting castles and shady river scenes. It was a silent place where pictures and paintings stared from the walls and muted volunteers smiled from the corners. There were no interactive displays or flashing lights — it was not the kind of collection that attracted schoolchildren. Its images, of what people thought the Rhine should have been, will stay, tucked away in a back street, and with each passing year will become more and more of an antique curiosity, an historical interpretation of romance.

I returned back along the Mosel, crossed the Rhine and climbed to the hostel which was again situated in a castle overlooking the city. This time the fortress was the redoubtable Festung Ehrenbreitstein, one of the oldest strongholds on the river. Used by the Romans as a signal outpost, the first recorded traces of a fortress at the site are in the sixth century, and Ehrenbrecht, the builder of the current incarnation, believed that from that one strategic location he could control the traffic on both rivers.

The castle has survived the Rheinland's tribulations and its reputation as indomitable remained intact until 1801, when the French blew the bastion sky-high with 14,000 kilograms of gunpowder. The Prussians, after receiving the region in the Conference of Vienna, rebuilt it between 1815-32. Ehrenbreitstein endured another 140 years as an active military garrison before the advent of aerial bombing and the potential of atomic warfare resigned it to being a relic with a great view.

My room in the fortress had ten beds and a tiny window just large enough for an archer to poke his weapon through. My roommates that night were three friends from Seoul, Korea, a hyperactive trio who entered the room surrounded by a cloud of alcoholic fumes and laughter. One of them, in rose-tinted glasses and a chaos patterned T-shirt, immediately came up to me and introduced himself, "HELLO, my name is DANNY. What's yours, MAN?" His loud emphasis was motivated I guessed by the old adage, "If they don't understand, shout."

Danny, it turned out, spoke passable English, but his two friends were barely past the rudiments. Their inquiries were phrased along the lines of "You, in, Germany, how long, one, two day?" and "You like Europe, we like much, much."

We sat together and had a group conversation about me, a dialogue from which I was curiously excluded. Danny interpreted for his disciples what he thought I was thinking, without bothering to ask for my opinion. It was like having people talk about you behind your back, while you stared at them. I left, which didn't seem to bother the trio as they were still absorbed in discussing me in the first person.

When I returned the boys were undressed down to underwear and socks, white cotton briefs accompanied by blue or black polyester stockings of the kind that come to mid-calf and never drop below that. They had arranged themselves in a disciplined line and were practicing tae kwon do positions, synchronized Bruce Lee clones, the three of them erupting together in ear-splitting shrieks.

When they saw me, they stopped in mid-move and Danny came running over to apologize. "Most sorry, Jono, but we are almost naked. Sorry for this inconvenience." I didn't think of it as any kind of inconvenience, just strange.

They put their jeans back on and returned to their huddle. After awhile Danny came to the table on which I was writing and, out of the blue, said, "Jono, Korea is like Germany, very many castles, SO romantic. Are you enjoying the romance here on the Rhine?" I replied, half apologetically, that I wasn't really looking for romance on the river.

With this Danny returned, somewhat dejectedly, to his comrades, and their conversation was hushed for the rest of the evening. Now I was confused. Was I boarding with a group of gay vagabond Koreans, or just with a troupe of happy-go-lucky young men, trying hard to make the Rhine fit the standards that they had built for it? Soon I fell asleep, and in the morning there was no sign of Danny or his friends.

North again. Now the farms were less frequent and the villages were packed tighter and tighter. Old houses, their weathered timbers lovingly painted to cover time's destructive hand, sat beside concrete mansions, their driveways bristling with shiny vehicles.

High-water marks on the antique waterfront homes were indicative of an increasing number of exceptional floods in this century. Was this due to diminishing forests higher up in the Alps, or some consequence of the greenhouse effect? Either way the marks did not compare to the unreachable heights that the Ganga had been registered at on walls in Varanasi. I took it as an indication that at least in the European mountains some plant life still survives.

Remagen was my next stop. I was excited, as it is the site of my one notable childhood Rhine memory, and that one Rheinisch reminiscence courtesy of Hollywood.

I can still envision that final scene from *A Bridge Too Far,* where the American GI lies on the Ludendorff Bridge as the Nazi officer presses the lever to blow the span to kingdom come. As the smoke of the explosion clears, we get a shot of the same soldier, shocked at the fact that the bridge is still standing.

There is truth to Hollywood's interpretation of March 7, 1945. The bridge miraculously survived the retreating Wehrmacht's attempt at demolition and stood for another ten days, letting a nonstop stream of Allied forces cross the ultimate boundary into the German heartland. With the breaching of the Rhine, Hitler's last great defensive position and the psychological border between "us" and "them" was shattered. Germany's river became Allied territory and the Second World War was all but over.

From Remagen it's less than twenty-five kilometers to Bonn, Germany's temporary capital. With the reunification of west and east, Bonn, the capital for the past forty years, is being supplanted by Berlin. I found it strange for me to think of Bonn as the administrative center during the days of the thriving Federal Republic. It is a quiet town, obviously the home of conservative bureaucrats and retirees, and consequently possessed by none of the cosmopolitan flair of cities such as Berlin or Paris or London. But possibly, on that fateful day in 1948, when the postwar parliamentary council gathered for its first session amongst the stuffed creatures in Alexander König's biological museum, it was a good choice.

Bonn was one of the few cities in the Rhine area not completely demolished by Allied air raids. It was strategically placed close to the heart of German industry, yet held a tranquil position on the Rhine. All around it cities were caught in the chaotic throes of reconstruction. It had peace, it had history and it had the Rhine — all the items that the new Germany needed.

The temporary capital lingered, and Bonn stayed on as the capital for four decades, until another explosion, this time to the east, reunited the Germanic tribes and retrieved Berlin as its true home city. I have to wonder if history will record it as a period like that of the Pope's exile to Avignon, as an anomalous blip on the timeline of irregular expatriations.

To me, Bonn lived up to its mandate as temporary. Although it is endowed with a rich array of fine national museums and galleries, the Bundestag, the meeting place of the German government, was a fleeting attempt at crossing Norman Foster with portable classrooms. The Bundestag was definitely not there to stay.

Bonn's time as a center of power had come and gone, and as I pedaled along a well laid out network of bike paths, no doubt part of a national capital beautification scheme, I looked north. Both banks were flanked with tree-lined trails and populated with an inordinate amount of old people walking small dogs. There was nothing out of the ordinary. Bonn would quickly revert back to what it historically had been, a quiet city, attractive to the retired, a bastion of tradition and uniformity.

The river north of Bonn takes its time, any rush to reach the ocean lost in the flatness of the earth around it. The landscape opens out and its wide meanders give the flow a lazy, sauntering continence.

I passed the Degussa plant, another all-purpose manufactory like BASF, one of the world's few dozen raw material mega-producers. Its skyline was a jumble of chimneys and geometric roofs, and above it hovered ominous clouds of steam. Each chimney emitted a different colored strata, evidence of the transformations taking place in the factory's bowels. In the unexpected noon sunlight the thick vapors painted the sky in a blurred, industrial watercolor.

I stopped for lunch in the shadow of its smokestacks and, as I was putting together another cheese and tomato sandwich, a man on a bicycle stopped for a chat. Eric Fram was in his mid-forties, an office worker whose heavy body was tucked into a matching set of lycra tights and shirt. It was obvious that he was fighting the battle of the waistline, and everyday, he told me, he rode his $4,000 mountain bike out to that spot. It was an offensive action in the war with his body.

He was a pleasant man; we talked for an hour or so about bikes, cameras, and his experiences with the river that he rode beside daily. They were manly subjects, about objects and how to use them, and experiences with the objects you had mastered. When I suggested that he go to North America for a larger bike tour, he shrugged, and almost shyly said that it was his dream, but since he suffered from claustrophobia it was an impossibility. For him when the door closed on an airplane he felt so out of control that he would rather jump from the window than put on the seatbelt. Our conversation stalled, and then he looked at the river and said, "You know, the Rhine is like the opening of those doors for North Germany. It is the outlet for the claustrophobia of our cramped society."

There was truth in Eric's image. The Rhineland-Westphalia region is the manufacturing heartland of Germany, with people and industry

147

packed together with asphyxiating density. The great desire for most is space, lebensraum, room to move and live and breathe. The river, to Eric, provided that freedom — it was the channel that drew away the pent up energy, released the frustrations of those millions, and let them continue on in civilized normality.

In the distance I could barely make out the spires of the Cologne cathedral, two gray, pencil-thin rockets, dominating the flattened, squared-off vista of the city. The great church was my target, as it must have been for travelers 750 years ago. That a building begun in the thirteenth century was able to command the skyline seven centuries later made it even more enticing. The cathedral was magnetic architecture.

As I pulled into the downtown core the sky blackened and a drizzle greeted me, not a dampening downpour but a silent, sopping mist that made the city shimmer in the glow of internally generated light. I was riding through the city electric.

I crossed one of the many bridges to the right bank suburb of Deutz and from there found my way to the hostel. That night I had dinner with a Dutch woman who was doing consumer surveys in a dozen North German cities and we talked about Holland, Germany and Europe.

I was interested in the way that she talked about Europe in the first person plural, "We Europeans. . . ." To her the continent was united in its diversity — the British fighting the union from their island home were "isolationist" and the Swiss, who refused to budge on their centuries' old policy of neutrality, were "strange." She peppered the conversation with statements like "We will move together into the next millennium" and "We will always be regionally different." It was my first meeting with the potentially homogenous future of the continent.

The next day I made my way back across the bridge to the cathedral. What I had seen in the darkness of the night before had not done it justice. In the daylight I saw it for what it was, a masterpiece, the crowning achievement in the string of cathedrals that I had traced from as far back as Basel.

Cologne, the largest, richest city on the Rhine, was also in possession of its most powerful piece of architecture. The church was surrounded by dozens of modern and post-modern artistic fantasies, temples to art and history. But they paled in comparison to the building that was not just larger and more detailed in its work, but was so steeped in faith and narrative that its mammoth proportions and disproportions dissolved inwards.

The cathedral is built on a low hill a hundred meters from the Rhine, a position that until the intense building of the past two centuries must have offered one of the area's few unobstructed views of the river. The site had previously housed a Roman temple, an early sixth-century Christian church, and the ninth-century Carolingian Cathedral of Hildebold. But in 1164 the sepulcher of the "three Magi," the three wisemen of the nativity, was brought to the city and a new and more suitable building was planned to hold the relics. By the time construction started in 1248 Cologne had already experienced a long and illustrious history. The construction of such an awe-inspiring structure could not have been undertaken without a powerful ecclesiastical community and a fourishing economy.

The site of Cologne was chosen by the Romans to settle their Germanic allies, the Ubii, and by 50 CE Colonia Claudia ara Agrippinensium had gained imperial colonial status, and thus its name, from the Teutonic transliteration of the Latin "Colonia." This initiated a four hundred year period of prosperity that ended when the Franks drove the Romans from the city. Slowly Cologne rebuilt itself until by 800 the emperor Charlemagne had raised the city to an archbishopric.

The city was well-placed at the junction of the Rhine and a multitude of international trade routes. Cologne became a member of the Hanseatic League and, using the river to its advantage, traded as far away as Sicily and Scandinavia. The cathedral was the high mark of this second period of prosperity, but the construction was a drawn out process and in 1560 it came to a grinding halt.

Uncertainty within and the eventual disintegration of the Holy Roman Empire left the church in a state of disrepair for more than three hundred years. But in the nineteenth century a resurgence of interest in the Middle Ages and Gothic art, the same movement that had fostered the Romantics, swept across Europe and brought a renewed desire to complete the cathedral.

With the coming of the Industrial Revolution Cologne again rode a wave of affluence and the realization of the church became a focus for the entire community, a point of pride to testify to the world that Cologne was in the vanguard of the new wave of urban Meccas. Kaiser Freidrich Wilhelm IV laid the foundation for the resumption of construction and, faithfully following the thirteenth-century master plans, the great enterprise was completed in 1880.

But the winds of fortune once more blew against the church and its city. During World War Two, in the Allied air raids of 1942-45, over 75 percent of Cologne was destroyed, and the cathedral, although it survived, was badly damaged. The Kölners pulled themselves up by the bootstraps, and by the '60s the city's reconstruction was complete, with the cathedral yet again taking pride of place amongst a bevy of new architectural baubles.

It was intriguing to see the juxtaposition of old and new. The cathedral had taken one hundred times as long to build as its neighbors. Its architect must have had a true artist's faith to believe that his vision could, in some distant century, reach fruition.

I wondered, if they had had that faculty, what the new glass and steel galleries have thought of their dominating grandfather. Did they look at the cathedral with stony-eyed jealousy, and did they wish, in a dense, inorganic way, that they too would reach the age of 750 and instill such feeling?

I stood at the base of the church trying to appreciate its scale. The size was put into perspective by the replicas, lying near the main entrance, of the fluted blooms that crown its spires. They are massive stone details, larger than me, and yet their real life relatives, perched atop the 187-meter steeples, looked like tiny insects buzzing the peaks of distant summits. I felt insignificant.

Then across the cathedral square hundreds of revelers appeared, all dressed in festive costumes, singing, shouting and bonding in alcoholic fraternity. I was witnessing Cologne's other outlet for pent up urban pressure — carnival. During the year there are over four hundred different festival events, all culminating in the annual Rose Monday parade. As I watched the square filled with ecstatic, wildly attired revelers and the plain drunk. Songs erupted sporadically, and mugs of beer were passed around freely.

Above us floated the cathedral, the gargoyles, with their hunched backs and squinting eyes, smiled, and the wispy spires caught shafts of sunlight and threw them, gnarled and twisted, down amongst the carousers. The thought occurred to me of what the Three Magi would think if they saw what was happening on their front doorstep.

One group came over and offered me a glass of frothy brew. How could I refuse? As I entered their circle arms came over my shoulders and much to their amusement I tried to join in the drinking songs. The group pulled and cajoled me out of the square and off to a beer garden on the riverbank.

I pedaled out of the city towards Dusseldorf. The area became more and more saturated with industry. The Ford plant in Longerich and the Bayer factory in Dormagen stood out for their monolithic scale. I was entering the Ruhr, the rusting homeland of German heavy industry.

The Ruhr region extends for one hundred kilometers along the Rheinisch tributary from which it takes its name, and for fifty kilometers along the Rhine itself. It has a long history of iron smelting but it wasn't until 1837 that the area started to intensively develop the industries it has become synonymous with. In that year technicians succeeded in drilling through the river valley's deep, sandy geology to strike rich veins of high quality coal. At the same time the Industrial Revolution was revamping the steel industry, and with the advent of coke-fed blast furnaces dramatically increased production became possible. In the Ruhr steel producers set up next to the coal suppliers and the entire area turned into a heavy industry conglomerate. It was the first of its kind in the world, a densely packed geographic space in which all manner of raw materials were transformed into finished products.

Steel production requires large amounts of raw materials which in turn demand an extensive transportation network. The coal was on the manufacturer's doorstep, but the ore, originally brought in from other parts of Germany or Alsace, was of too low a grade for the improved techniques. Thus, new supplies of higher grade iron ore were found in Sweden. The higher margins and the coinciding decrease in coke consumption led to more profits and, ultimately, to a hundred-year expansion of the Ruhr's heavy industry.

The Rhine played an indispensable role in the region's growth. It was the natural corridor for Scandinavian ore to be brought in, and the empty barges were easily filled with Ruhr coal or finished products for the downriver trips. Without the Rhine and the flow of ideas that are the inevitable byproduct of a well-traveled trade route, the Ruhr's astonishing growth would have been only a dream.

Dusseldorf loomed ahead of me. In the distance I could see the city tower, a blinking, space age mace wrapped in neon. In the foreground stood a tremendously fundamental looking coal-fired power station, its antediluvian chimneys dwarfing the techno-tower to its rear.

Dusseldorf was the first Rhine city whose riverfront I found depressing. As the marketable romance of the Rhine has brought cities to revamp their waterfronts, the business of heavy industry has been replaced by the business of tourism and real estate.

I arrived from the south and rode through an industrial area of blown-out warehouses, derelict factories and rusting rail tracks. From within the shipping houses a ceaseless line of roaring transport trucks attested to the fact that the neighborhood was still alive and working. I had to remind myself that that waterfront bustle was what had built those cities, and without the river Dusseldorf would have remained a second-rate center, renowned more for beer and sausage than manufacturing.

When I reached the downtown I found myself again surrounded by carnival revelers. The crowds sang songs and swayed back and forth in a style that I associated with TV interpretations of Germany. The smell of sizzling bratwurst and spilling tankards of lager filled the air. I stopped for a beer, thankful for my neighbors' outlandish attire and therefore not so self-conscious about my smell or mud-spattered cycling gear.

The beer was good and I struck up a conversation with the man beside me, an overweight burgher in a leather cowboy outfit. He spoke good English and took it upon himself to be my conduit to carnival culture. However, he was drinking twice as fast as I, and after a couple more mugs his explanations of carnival idiosyncrasies disintegrated into personal displays of some of those features.

His most poignant quote of the evening had to do with the refreshment he was downing so fast. He said, "My friend, we Ruhrlanders are known for our ability to work. Ja? Well, work makes you thirsty. Ja? And through this beer," and he pointed at his half filled mug, "that thirst will become an adventure." In his staggering state, I thought that the carnival night's greatest adventures would take place in his dreams.

The next morning I followed the Rhine's eastern dike system north towards Duisburg. I was impressed and depressed at how planned the Ruhrisch landscape was, as urban areas retreated into green belts, which gave way to industry. It was a pattern that repeated with all too obvious consistency. There was a scheme there, a plan to separate the people from their work and throw a corridor of contrived nature between them. To my utopian eyes it was too fabricated, and I had to console myself with the thought that it was at least a step beyond the nineteenth century's unreserved industrialization.

For a long time I rode beside the fenced-off water treatment grounds of the Dusseldorf municipal works. It was a long, winding meadow of well-tended grass scattered with the odd ornamental tree, more reminiscent of a golf course than a purification plant. But the quality of the city's water demanded it, because drinking water in this part of the country has to be double filtered. First the river water is naturally processed through the gravel and sand layers of the Rhine's banks and after some days or weeks, the semi-filtered product is pumped into the purification plant and processed again through gravel and active charcoal filtration.

The problem with this method, as highlighted by the Sandoz spill in Basel, is that without rigorous administration, the shores may become so saturated with toxins that bank filtration will become impossible.

By the water meadow I had the pleasure of having my first and only meeting with an urban shepherd. I was standing by my bike staring at the marine traffic, when down the dike path, moving at an almost imperceptible pace, came a turquoise, early '60s Volkswagen Beetle. Engulfing it to the rear were a hundred or so sheep, freshly sheared, their backs painted with red Xs, moving as a single unit, an organic wave borne on four hundred legs. The pool of bald animals was held in check by a pair of raffish sheepdogs. The dogs raced tirelessly amongst the flock, cajoling the sheep and nipping at their ankles with an enthusiasm that betrayed their joy in life.

In the car a man, well into his fifties, reclined in the front seat, a huge Father Christmas beard wrapped around his beaming smile and a narrow-brimmed loden hat topping his hairy, heavily wrinkled face. As he pulled alongside he shouted hearty greetings to me, his beard opening like a chalk cave to expose a row of pearly teeth. Below the steering wheel I could see a bottle of beer sitting snugly between his legs. He caught my glance and offered me one from a crate in the rear seat. I gladly accepted and he, with some effortful grunts, released himself from the Beetle.

The urban shepherd opened the bottle with a Swiss army knife that looked to be permanently connected to his body by a leather thong. He handed me a beer, toasted me in some village dialect, and downed the contents of his tall boy in one. I was shocked and took a large swig so as to at least keep the pace. But with that singular action he reentered his Beetle and with shouts of "Grossgluck mein freund" rolled away, singing so loud that he drowned out the mechanical insect's air-cooled engine.

Behind him the sheepdogs barked out unordered commands and the sheep stayed glued to the antique jalopy. I was so impressed at this scene of unexpected *joie de vivre* that I put the half finished beer into my waterbottle holder and headed off in the opposite direction singing at the same volume as my southbound hero.

Soon I was moving into the suburbs of Duisburg, and it was obvious that the city had also felt the hand of the Second World War's destruction. All the houses were of newer brickwork, terracotta and white palaces sitting on tiny well-manicured plots. Even my passing glance could tell that they were solid constructions, built like their predecessors to last three hundred years. Earlier on my trip a man had told me how German families took out multigenerational mortgages to finance those mansions. The real estate was passed from parents to children, the family tied to the soil from one age to the next not by a cycle of seasons but by financial commitments.

Duisburg had been flattened during World War Two because it was the vital link, the transportation brain, between the Ruhr and the rest of the globe. The city is the largest river port in the world. For the Allies to shut down the Nazi war machine they had to sever its transportation network, and so Duisburg was sacrificed.

I was shocked when I wandered through the local museum and saw what the city had looked like before the long night of the early '40s. Its prewar tight, almost medieval, plan had expanded on the reconstruction into wide urban prairie of thoroughfares and expansive plazas. Some could call it violent progress, but there was pain in that forced change.

Maybe I saw it on the faces of the men I watched in Ruhrort, the city's northern extension. There the harbor is at its most animated, its most impressive. You can stand on the bridges and look out at the hive of activity clouding the smoggy skyline, cranes working overtime, back and forth, up and down, loads being shifted and transferred. It is interminable, unceasing.

I watched as old men, not one but dozens, walked slowly along the riverside path looking whimsically on at the hustle, the collars of their long overcoats turned up against the wind, stogies smoking between their lips. They were transfixed by the mechanical movement of the arms and buckets, the surging outbursts from the boats. What were they thinking behind those melancholy eyes? Were they trying to discern something in the swaying pallets and spilling armloads? Were they feeling what the operator felt? Was this a vicarious chance to relive a time when they were an integral part of all that they viewed, or were they merely feeling time slip by like the river at their feet?

I too was caught by that endless motion. There was a strange romanticism to the movement of goods and its relationship to some monetary transaction somewhere far away. Jakarta, Santiago, Lagos and Duisburg were all part of the same whole. Such globally interconnected activity was daunting. So much movement focused. A thousand tributaries a million types of goods, solid, liquid and gaseous, all feeding into the greater flow. The Rhine, as always, was the focus and product of infinite amounts of energy.

Yet Duisburg, I discovered the next day, was just the tip of this megalopolitan iceberg, for the Ruhr's urban sprawl goes on and on. Derelict lands merge with residences which interconnect with the factories which themselves lead to the river and eventually become absorbed by it. There was something subliminally attractive about the seemingly haphazard planning. It felt like a strange natural expansion of the local industry's imperialistic power. With the factories dominating the landscape there was no doubt what the population was focused on.

On the road I was trapped in a flow of traffic that pulled me from the waterfront, but it didn't matter as the bank had been given over to a string of industrial fiefdoms. Thyssen Stahl AG stood out, its smoking stacks and humungous steam-belching production houses made the sky a dark watercolored blur. The misty *mise en scène* turned into a comedy when the factory became the background for a roadside advertising board featuring someone in impossibly bright yellow holding a package of cigarettes while declaring, "Smoke your own style."

Hamborn was the only town along the river that appeared truly neglected. It was a gray-on-gray landscape, with a layer of soot adding depth to its ashen despair. The town looked to be predominantly Turkish, with the shops claiming "Dadas Imports" and "English Queen Fashions." I wondered if it was the German government who was reluctant to spend the money required to rescue the community from its destitution, or if the residents felt so temporary in this partly adopted land that they refused to adhere to the German idea of cleanliness.

From there it was on to Wesel and across to the river's western shore. The industrial landscape unlocked its grip just south of the town, and I was again moving through farmland. From mid-span on the Wesel bridge I looked out over the river and was surprised by the snaking lines of boats, so numerous now that occasionally they looked connected. They resmbled extra wide-gauge trains yoked from bow to stern. Around me the level of land had become so flat that the river seemed a logical extension of the earth, a murky gray highway, silent and more mysterious than its ashphalted counterparts.

On the west bank, near Birten, I stopped for lunch and was given a rude surprise. From the other side of the hedgerow I had moved behind to get out of the traffic and wind, I heard the screech of tires and the slamming of doors. Two men in plain clothes burst through the shrubs, barking earnest orders in German while flashing Stadt Poleizi key chains. "PASSE, JETZ!" They wanted my passport.

One man glared at me with his best imitation of the Prussian hard man, the vein above his temple bulging with each utterance. I handed my passport to his partner, the nice one in this "good cop, bad cop" scenario, while the "bad guy" shouted frantically, now in English, "ANY DRUGS?" I laughed, said no, and tried to explain that I was only there to see the Rhine. This didn't appear to help his mood and he told me to shut up while his partner went off to check my papers. I sat quietly as he glowered at me. I was his hostage, a potentially dangerous alien who had to be watched closely, and so we sat. I smiled, he frowned, and I wondered if he would ever be able to appreciate the river. Or would pleasure for him forever be contact sports and hard-core porn.

His partner returned with a pasted on smile and said with feigned politeness that everything was "OK." My inquisitor rose, a little dejectedly, and moved back to the car, crestfallen that he hadn't completed the bust. I was left behind the hedgerow with my now soggy cheese and tomato sandwich.

Xantan, five kilometers farther on, was my next stop. Xantan — the name clicks off the tongue with an exotic lisp, like Shambala or Xanadu. To the town's west the Festenburg hill rose stately above the floodplain, capped by its church and monastery, which were constructed from stone chiseled by pagan Romans. The town was draped in low fog, fitting, as its exoticism lies, not in the location, but in the mists of time. Xantan, from its Christianized name Ze Santen (to the saints), is most famous as the birthplace of the most German of German heroes, Siegfried of the thirteenth-century epic poem, the *Nibelungenlied*.

In more than thirty-nine adventures, in 2,300 verses, up and down the Rhine Siegfried battles dragons, evil henchmen, jealous maidens, lustful kings, armies of giants, and in the process becomes the archetypal Germanic hero. The poem mingles fact and fiction to create a figure that the National Socialists promoted as the epitome of the German male. Siegfrid was courageous, loyal, truthful, wise, and, because of the many powers he had acquired in his adventures, he could only be destroyed through the trickery of a former ally. But his legend lives on, and the belief that the treasures he had amassed are still unretrieved, lost at the bottom of the Rhine, is a topic of daily conversation in towns along its banks.

But centuries before Siegfrid's birth Xantan was heralded as Rome's most northerly continental outpost, the imperial dependency of "Colonia Ulpia Traiana." Xantan formed the endpoint of a border that shadowed the Danube and Rhine from the Black Sea to the English Channel. This was the famed Roman Limes, a 3,000 kilometer alignment of forts and colonies, pearls laced on the string of Romanesque polity, a riverine frontier that delineated the Roman from all else.

Colonia Ulpia Traiana was a fortified settlement of seventy hectares where 10,000 loyal Roman citizens made their homes. The archeological park just outside the town brought history home to me. The complexity of the society, the refinement of their living and the social structure that it was built upon were incredibly sophisticated. Looking at the excavated ruins, shards of worked stone and reconstructed fragments, I was numbed to think that it could all have so completely disappeared, disposed of by people unconcerned with recording their own history.

But that is what happened, for the empire imploded on its weakened core and in the third century succumbed to the might of a greater sword. The line that had been drawn along the two great rivers, the fluvial filament between the civilized and the infidel, collapsed. The psychological barrier that separated the Romans, with their matrix of culture and trade connecting Britain to Syria, was consumed by marauding hordes from the east and north, bands not desirous of education or wisdom, but plunder.

But the disintegration of the Limes is not without legacy, for the idea of a distinct border, a line drawn on maps more than on the earth, still haunts us. From decaying empires, to Bosnia and Kashmir we are driven to delineate what separates "us" and "them." For the Romans, and the French, and the Germans and who knows of the future, the river has been that border. Beyond these waters dragons lie.

From Xantan to Kleves I returned to the river along farmland, flat and industrious. There, for the first time, I caught sight of windmills, pushed by a wind blowing unobstructed from the North Sea, their blades carved gracefully on the horizon. At Kleves I halted for the night in a deserted hostel with a priceless view over the forest to the northeast.

Kleves is interesting as the home of two heroes, one immortalized far from the Rhine and another who never left home. Johanna Sebus was a 17-year-old girl who died while helping to shore up the dike system in the flooding of 1809. She would have passed as quietly as she had lived if she had not been immortalized in song by Goethe, and become the shadowy background for the legend of the girl with her finger in the dike.

The second mythological resident of Kleves is Lohengrin, the knight of the Holy Grail. In his quests he traveled to the far corners of the known world, but he returned to Kleves on the river and passed from this life along its banks. The world had captivated him but the river was his home. The Rhine, like all rivers, is a thread of memory for its waters connect the home and the away.

I woke the next day to a winter bright morning. The sun was a golden orange orb caught between vaporous bands of rising dew. I headed to the river, found the dike road and cycled it to Millingen. There I crossed another silent border, this time between Germany and Holland, and the only indication that I had traversed some civic boundary was the different language that appeared on the road signs.

For five kilometers before that I had ridden in an area where the flow was split between Germany on one bank and the Netherlands on the other. At Millingen I was completely in Holland and almost immediately the river bifurcated. The true, singular Rhine, as if lamenting its exit from the fatherland, was lost.

To the north flowed the Kromme Rijn, the Twisted Rhine, which passes the pilgrimage city of Utrecht, transforms to the Oude Rijn, runs through Leiden, and empties, as an anemic shadow of its former self, into the Atlantic at Katwijk. Directly west flows the more powerful

Waal, the river that branches and breaks and splits upon itself until its hundreds of offshoots and tributaries transform the southern Netherlands into what it is, the Rhine delta, a river world.

I followed it past Nijmegen, a city built around the only hill that I was to see in that planar nation. The topography was excruciatingly monotonous, a piece of the globe where water and earth are so easily intermixed that waterland is its best epithet.

A saying has it that God made the planet, but left Holland to be made by the Dutch themselves. The land is webbed with ditches, canals and man-altered rivers. This compulsion to direct water is a necessity that has become a passion. The Dutch have done everything physically possible to master the flow of the Rhine. Without this Holland would be consumed by the father flow and absorbed by the waiting ocean. It is a credit to the technicians and a necessary shame for the river.

After Nijmegan the Waal is paralleled by the Maas, another of the great European inland waterways. Where the rivers run together the world is green and misty, a horizontal landscape in which the earth is separated from the sky by only a stark gray line of deciduous trees.

This is the most intensively farmed land I have ever seen. Animals and new sprung cereals stared up from the ground. The atmo-sphere was thick with the smell of agricultural prosperity, manure, acrid and sharp, held in the air by a dense palpable moisture. But this is not a quiet land, and even here, away from the highway, the sound of divisions of tractors and combines and loaders and crawlers filled my ears. To cultivate this earth means to keep the land from the water, and to insure that the Dutch must be continually reworking their system of defenses.

Dike construction is an ongoing process, a labor that must pull the nationalism from the soul of every heavy equipment operator and in some way make him a small god. After all, it is his Caterpillar that is making the Netherlands a possibility.

I pushed hard onto Zaltbommel as the sun turned bloodred and receded to the flat lined horizon. There was no hostel, and the place was too populated for me to pitch a tent. I went to a gas station in search of coffee and asked a couple of truckers for directions to the next large town. One of them, a jovial guy with a gap-toothed smile and a well-grown salt and pepper beard, said with a heavy accent, "Don't worry, man, you can follow the river to Gorinchem. The moon will be full tonight, just keep your eyes open for mermaids and whales." He laughed, slapped me on the back, and offered me a coffee saying, "Twenty more kilometers, fella, you better take some more sugar."

And so I rode up onto the dike path and west. Behind me the moon hung over the extreme geometry of the E.25 freeway bridge. It was a creamy smooth disk softly lying against the hazard lights and halogens adorning the span. Before the sun set I looked to the river and watched the barges churn upstream, cutting water so thick that in the last long light of day it looked to be molasses.

With the sunset the arc of my bike light sliced a thin tunnel through the half-darkness, but the full moon was at my back and my shadow was centered within the lamp's glow. My wheels whirred on the asphalt, the countryside was quiet, the Caterpillars had gone to bed. I could hear the splash of fish jumping in the ditches and the cool swoosh of startled cranes as I moved soundlessly by. In the distance I heard the roar of spectators at a village football match and the distant thunder of highway trucks, but these were far off. For now I was engulfed in a melancholic reverie, a perceptible, almost vaporous noiselessness that stilled the mind and brought thought in. It was a cerebral environment much more the match for the silent, moonstruck river.

I reached Gorinchem sooner than I expected. I was having a wonderful night. For the first time since my initial glimpse at the source I felt alone and undisturbed, so I continued on into the night, passing blackened villages and silent towns until, near midnight, I reached Dordrecht. There I found a hostel and quickly fell to dreams in black and white.

Dordrecht was the port of destination for cargo moving down the Rhine during the time of the Hanseatic League. But I was too excited to give it its due, and the next morning I moved on with thoughts of the Atlantic filling my head.

The next stop was Rotterdam, an urban amoeba that spreads itself along the Nieuwe Maas for mile after mile. The history of Rotterdam, like its contemporaries in Germany, is a roller coaster tale of boom and bust. From a herring fishing village in the fourteenth century it developed into an international seaport in the second half of the sixteenth century. Then, with the change to iron clad steam ships in the nineteenth century, a complete renovation of the harbor was made, and the rapid growth in the Ruhr was mirrored in Rotterdam, the region's opening to the sea.

By the 1930s the harbor was rivaling New York in size, but then World War Two gripped the globe. In one day, May 14, 1940, Rotterdam was leveled in a series of air raids. By the end of the hostilities 25,000 houses, 2,350 shops and warehouses, 2,000 workshops and factories, 1,450 offices, 550 bars, 62 schools, 25 government buildings, 24 churches, 22 dance halls, 13 hospitals, 12 cinemas, and 2 theaters had been destroyed. The state of affairs in the city was so bad it was said that their amicable arch rivals, the Amsterdammers, even took pity on them. Yet it only took the city eight years to get its harbor back to prewar levels, an acheivement that almost defies comprehension.

The city of today is the product of that surge of fantastic activity. Rotterdam is the archetype of the postwar urban space, a planned and reconstructed city, so devoid of its own physical past that its history could all be a rumor. Here are buildings in stainless steel and concrete that match the chromed cement gray of the old river. It is a square in three dimensions, a modernist's dream, a place destined to become an icon for our century. But until history plays upon it, it will remiain a decipherable labyrinth of boulevards flanked by the ubiquitous shopping arcades and blocks of habitable squares. It is western Europe's one upmanship on Communist Russia's utilitarian architectural dreams.

But Rotterdam is most of all a city of the river, an entity produced by the Rhine and focused on that flow; without it Rotterdam would revert to herring fishing. The fact was brought home to me by the owner of the bookshop in the Maritime Museum.

He was a generous man, with a thick gray beard like those of the sailors pictured in his books. He insisted that I stay with him and his family that night, so we put my bicycle in his car and made the trek out to the suburbs. There we talked long into the night about the river and Rotterdam. With a glass of beer in his hand he admitted his fondness for the Rhine and eventually said, "Yes, we must love that gray and murky flow. We make money from it, we live by it, and we survive through it. We drink it everyday — whatever happens downstream in Germany and France and Switzerland ends up in our bodies. Whether we like it or not, Rotterdammers are made of the Rhine."

From Rotterdam to the ocean man has created his own Rhine, the 20-meter deep and 12-kilometer long Nieuwe Waterweg. It is a larger version of the river engineering I had seen in Vorarlberg and Alsace, but here the sense of human control is taken to the extreme. At one point a set of massive gates, kilometers wide, sits to one side of the waterway. In a matter of minutes they can be moved across the stream to increase or decrease the flow. They are the hands of some god of logic, halting the river's progress in the name of survival. The survival of the Netherlands.

The waterway is lined with oil refineries. Rotterdam is the world's oil marketplace. This stretch of the river is known as Euorport, the largest seaport and the greatest concentration of petroleum refineries in the world. It is the place that fuels the fantasies of a world addicted to the internal combustion engine.

When I was there the refineries were shaded by a seashore fog. Dim, triangulated outlines were barely visible, but a line of thin chimneys flaring with shots of refining remnants burned through the mist. The chimney flames appeared diabolical in the distant light. They were floating fires hovering above unknown ground. It was *Dante's Inferno* brought to the North Sea.

The bike path followed through the towns of Vlaardingen and Maaslius and ended in the Hoek van Holland. There I watched a gargantuan high speed catamaran take an incredible line of cars and trucks into its belly, close its doors, and soundlessly pull away for England.

It was the lack of noise that impressed me. The ferry was moving between nations, yet there was no fanfare, no confetti showers or brass bands. At the end of the Rhine, with no land in sight, it was as if borders had disappeared.

Just north of the town I parked my bike and walked into a wild set of wind-battered sand dunes. It was a fitting passage to the ocean — gorse and heather hung onto life in an almost uninhabitable environment. As at Dry Bay and Ganga Sagar, this is where the river ends its gifting flow. This is where it stops depositing its silt and soils and pushing the frontiers of land. In that malleable landscape, beyond the permanence that we want to feel in the earth at our feet, I could truly appreciate the river. The river is time and space, it is the movement that we all intuitively appreciate, but can never touch. The river is the flow that moves through us to our children and back to our parents. It is the entity that moves the world and provides us with life. The river is in us all.

From the summit of one of those sandy hills I looked out at the sea. Whitecapped waves raced across the surface and pounded the shore, and the wind, thick with salt and spray, blew through me to the bone. For my landlocked mind there was nothing out there but pure emptiness. The sea was the great void, the place we cannot touch and yet all know. The Rhine moved into it silently and without complaint. The river was going home.

Tatshenshini

High up in the spruce trees on river right I saw a single raven stop its fastidious grooming and stare down at us as we floated noiselessly past its perch. The raven cocked its head in a questioning motion, possibly confused by the sight of such an otherworldly craft drifting through its world. Or perhaps, considering what lay just ahead, it was bewildered by our group's nonchalance.

Downriver I could hear the sound of rapids and leaned over to secure my cameras. Rising I looked ahead and my mouth dropped in dumbfounded surprise. We were into the teeth of the rapids and the raft was on the crest of a four meter standing wave.

The boat hung for a millisecond on the wave's thrashing lip, and then, like a roller coaster diving for the candy stalls, hurtled into the trough. I grabbed the closest safety line and the obscenity that left my lips was lost to the river's roar.

As the boat bottomed out the world around us became a churning wall of water and I looked back to see Adam in the throes of a laughing fit. He was loving everything about this surprise.

Looking beyond him, over his left shoulder, I saw the preening raven flying low to the water. Its head was turned in our direction, its beak open and cackling. It too was caught in the comedy of my fright. The raven was laughing at me.

Two and a half weeks earlier Andy's old '72 Volkswagen bus had sat disabled on the side of the Alcan Highway, its back axles supported by rocks, its wheels removed to expose the rusty brakedrums.

We — Andy, Adam and myself — were heading for the source of the Tatshenshini River when the van had had an explosive flat tire halfway between Whitehorse, Yukon, and Haines, Alaska. The microbus had careened to an uncontrolled stop on a sparking steel rim and we had all tumbled out to stare at the smoking wheel.

Pulling the canvas cover off the spare tire we'd discovered that it too was airless. Bad luck and bad planning were conspiring against us. Andy, the owner of the bus, was nominated to take the tires back to Whitehorse while Adam and myself stayed behind to nurse our crippled chariot.

A steady stream of Arctic-bound semitrailers had blasted past us, rocking the unsteady van and threatening to knock it from its temporary supports. The swirling breezes passed us by and continued on into the woods. Scores of aspen leaves instantly broke into spontaneous trembling fits. The shaking of a million leaves is a disconcerting sound; it has the same low, private whisper of conspiratorial laughter.

Tatshenshini, in the language of the Tutchone, the inhabitants of its headwaters, means "river of the raven." The raven in coastal native culture is the mythological trickster. While stranded on the side of the highway, inundated with the sound of the forest, it felt as if the raven river was chuckling at our folly.

We were headed for the Tatshenshini's wellspring, into the largest non-polar ice cap in the world, a region that extends from the northwest corner of British Columbia into the Yukon and Alaska. This long-limbed glacial spider connects the hundreds of cirques and valleys that stretch along the North American Coast Mountains, a range that extends from California almost to the Arctic.

Our goal was to traverse that mountain system by hiking and rafting the one watercourse, the Tatshenshini River, that has eroded a path through its highest and most inhospitable region. The source lies in British Columbia's Tatshenshini Wilderness Preserve. It flows north into the Yukon's Kluane National Park and then turns 180 degrees. It reenters the wilderness preserve and crosses the international border into Alaska's Glacier Bay National Park before eventually dispersing itself into the Pacific. Thus the 254 kilometers of the Tatshenshini are completely surrounded by an international park system. The Tatshenshini is the largest preserved river system in the world.

For me the Tat represented the river in its most primal form. The Tatshenshini's natural history is a living example of what rivers were before humankind invented the tools to control them. It is a river removed from hydropower and intensive irrigation, an untamed entity that determines the fate of all who follow its course.

Two hours after repairing the flat tire we were climbing the Chilkat Pass that separates the U.S and Canada.

The forested valley had given way to meagre brush-covered hillsides. Not much farther up the mountain slopes I could make out the band of rock that marked where plant life surrendered to the high alpine.

We topped a hillock and looked down upon a wide stoney basin pockmarked with stunted trees and thin swamp grasses. To the east was Kelsall Lake, whose river empties south into the Pacific. Not far to the north was the Takhini River whose waters run to the Arctic. To the west was the Datsalaska Range where the Tat originates. It was a landscape of choices, a good place to begin our journey.

We pulled into a gravel pit just south of Datsalaska Creek. The old air-cooled microbus was smoking from the climb. Ahead a long ridge was decapitated by low clouds, while behind us Kelsall Lake caught the sun's obtuse glow and shone like a silver plate in an earth-tone hollow. Around us the landscape was crumbling. Paleozoic sedimentary rock, sandy and loose, was falling away, eaten by creeks and scoured by the wind. The land felt transient, a place in constant movement.

We followed the creek into the hills and it made a long arc around a dun colored mountain. We crossed the intersecting ridge, climbing out of the Sitka alder thickets and into thin alpine grass. From the ridge we looked down and saw the creek split by the boulders dropped in its path. Its flow became a set of metallic ribbons slicing through an ephemeral gravel valley.

On the mountains to the south I saw a family of mountain goats making its way across a cliff face, their steps delicate leaps around an ever present abyss. The nanny and three kids skipping across the scarp were a display of the most fluid motion, every step calculated and perfectly executed. Their progress along the cliff's simplest line was an acrobatic interpretation of the river's own winding path through the hills.

As we edged around the ridge the first of the Tat's source glaciers became visible, a crooked apron of dirty summer snow cradled between two peaks. From its tongue a thin stream of water, churned white by the steep descent, dropped to the valley. A few hundred meters more and the primary glacier came into view, set majestically at the head of a U-shaped valley.

For its first five hundred meters the icefield lay at a low angle and its surface looked surprisingly uncut by crevasses. Farther on, the ice climbed sharply and was wrinkled with the fissures that cut apart its massive body. From it two subsidiary streams fell away on the left and right.

The right hand flow originated close to the ridge top, issuing from a hidden source and appearing halfway down the slope as a thick rusty, agitated effluent. The left hand creek was a slower murky brown. It was fed by the melting ice of the main glacier and entered the world from a dark, widemouthed cave at the ice floe's base.

We descended back to the river. The banks were blooming with bright pink, broad-leafed willow herb. The flowers bordered the creek almost the entire way to the ice cave. Like the flowery border on a springtime avenue they lent a subtle, feminine air to the muscular landscape.

Reaching the glacier we found its leading edge a mass of convoluted rock and dirt, a concretion pushed before its forward blade. Higher up, the ice was sun-cupped and rough, abrasive, yet slick. In every direction the ice was ripped by thin crevasses. None was more than a couple of feet in width, but they wove the surface like an icy web, evidence of the glacier's sluggish march. Surface water gathered and dropped into the fissures, polishing the crevasse walls to a glassy sheen that vibrated with an inner light. Through these frozen caverns the water charged, as if anxious to leave the lethargy of its solid form. What I saw in them was an icy birth canal. The solid was turning to liquid, the river's creation was in process.

The water cannoned along the channels, dropping in sets of sprayless waterfalls, disappearing into the blue blackness with a muffled roar. Those million trickles were on their way to joining a multitude of similar streams, all impatient to form a river. It was water through water, like the blood coursing through our own fluid bodies.

At lunch we headed for the lone rock on that tilted sea of ice. The stone caused a shadow to fall beneath it and there the ice had melted at a slower rate. The result was the rock teetering like a monstrous mushroom cap on a polished silver stem.

From our toadstool picnic spot we watched the sun break through the low hanging clouds and dance on the glacier's uneven floor. In random sweeps the surface exploded from a dull, shaly gray to titanium white, the spectrum moving in wide swathes like a celestial floodlight.

After our meal we left the frozen world and struggled through chest-high alders back down the creek's north bank. The clouds had finally dropped onto us, saturating the vegetation which in turn left its moist mark on us. I was soaked, and the chill sent a shiver through me. Water was everywhere: trapped in the glacier behind us, racing to the ocean in the river below, and hovering in the mist that floated between the realms.

We continued west until the gravel lot came into view. The sight of the van, with its dry clothes and heat, was a welcome one. Andy pulled the bus out onto the Haines highway and headed north, back into the Yukon.

The marshy tundra south of Kelsall Lake is fed by the Datsalaska and other tributaries. The high altitude, poor drainage and cold air rolling down off the surrounding glaciers have created an arctic ecosystem where scrub trees survive only on the best of growing sites.

Behind us lay the scattered remains of Glacier Camp, one of the stopover points on the historic Dalton Trail, a route that at the end of the last century wound its way 645 kilometers north, from Haines to Fort Selkirk and on down the Yukon River to the Klondike gold fields. Yet even twenty years before the Goldrush of 1898 the creation of such a trail would have been impossible. The routes to the interior were fiercely protected by the Tlingit native nations, the middlemen between white coastal traders and the inland, fur-trapping Tutchone people.

The Tlingits held the trading monopoly through most of the nineteenth century, but by the 1890s they were so decimated by imported European diseases that their position had collapsed. The opening of the Dalton and Chilkoot Trails and the onset of the goldrush marked the beginning of the end for autonomous Yukon native culture and the decline of the Tatshenshini as a trade route.

Jack Dalton, the frontier entrepreneur who pioneered the route, was the consummate American man of all trades, a seaman, cowboy, guide, and gunfighter. He had come with the first exploratory mission to the Chilkat in 1885 and had returned often until, a decade later, he had carved his own toll route out of the bush. Dalton charged between two dollars and $2.50 a head to use his trail, a price that seems to have been little debated, either because it was a fair price or because of Dalton's reputation with a gun.

But it was a difficult route originally. It crossed forty-eight kilometers of icefields, and traversed a pair of high passes before dropping into the Tatshenshini and Dezadeash watersheds that lead to the Yukon River. However, its more gentle grade, especially from the Pacific side, made it the preferred conduit for livestock, and the trail became one of the Klondike's primary food supply routes.

The old microbus crossed out of the Kelsall bowl, back over a set of hills and followed a river that grew more distinct with the meeting of each new tributary. This was the river that we could now call the Tat.

From the east the Blanchard River flowed to meet its larger cousin, and the highway made a slow curve left to follow its course. At the border between B.C. and the Yukon we pulled into a tidy highway maintenance yard. It looked and felt out of place so far removed from the company of other architecture. On the bank below the cinder block and corrugated steel workshop lay a ramshackle whitewater rafting camp. This was the seasonal home of a new breed of people whose livelihood was dependent upon the river. The salmon, trade and spiritual comfort that the river had provided the Tutchone has been replaced by the cash economy of adventure tourism.

It was deserted when we arrived. But around 10 p.m., with the sun still high in the northern sky, Jeff and Dan, the two resident guides, returned from some after dinner kayaking. Their neoprene wetsuits were still glistening from the river water and over their shoulders were slung the short, sleek kayaks that transformed them from land borne mammals to amphibians.

The little boats looked awkward when trapped on land, streamlined Tupperware containers, more useful for storing vegetables than inducing a metamorphosis. But water was their catalyst. When they touched the river, the hull changed from a receptacle to an appendage of the human body. By wearing that plastic sheathing and using it to feel the river surging around them, the kayakers became inhabitants of that element that permeates our innermost dreams.

175

After some food we made a fire and sat drinking beer, comfortable with the alcohol and warmth. The experienced kayakers settled into a discussion on the adventures of the day. The talk was of holes and sweepers, eddies and sieves. In their minds the river had a personality of its own, a chaotic but ordered nature that had to be experienced to be interpreted.

For me they were speaking a foreign language, the ghetto talk of fluvial mechanics. I felt estranged, a novice without expression. The men around me knew the water and how to describe its idiosyncrasies in specific ways, and yet, since I was trusting them to lead me down the river, their incomprehensible dialect represented a point of comfort for me, a sign of unknown knowledge.

The next morning I woke early. The Blanchard River was fifty meters from my sleeping bag and I went to wash. The air temperature was colder than that of the water, and on the river steam was rising. Long phantom wisps moved subtly with the draught created by the current. Above, rotund peaks were shrugging off the mists of dawn, revealing a rolling escarpment perforated by light and shadow. The clouds parted, slowly letting the sun warm the shaded valley.

I knelt to wash my face. Throwing the frigid water over me, I shuddered, the soap bringing tears to my eyes. I rinsed again and looked up to see a deer on the far shore, sipping water and pawing at the grass. I tried not to move, controlling my breathing, and it lingered, eyes to the water, entranced by its mirror image in a backeddy. Then, startled by the roar of a gravel truck, it instinctively threw its head back, and with a twitch, in one clean motion, it leapt, turned ninety degrees in the air, and was gone.

Over breakfast the conversation returned to water, but water from a business sense. The guides talked with Adam about the lines they would follow to get their commercial rafts safely to Dalton Post. Jeff and Dan both worked for Tatshenshini Expediting, a whitewater rafting outfit based in Whitehorse. That day they were expecting a contingent of clients for a trip through some of the Tat's toughest water. The guides had spent so much time on the river that for them it was almost second nature. Their discussion was to initiate Adam, our guide, into the Tatshenshini's more tempestuous moods.

As the least experienced guide on that section, he had been designated to transport the group's food and safety supplies. Adam's raft would be a double-hulled, inflatable catamaran, lighter and more easily maneuverable than the wide-bodied crew rafts. His secondary cargo would be Andy and myself, non-paddlers along for a free ride.

The plan sounded great until we realized that the cat only had one seat. Andy and I would be straddling the pontoons, like whitewater bareback riders. I sat down on the tube, which felt hard and smooth between my legs. My position would be tenuous — only the clutch of my inner thighs would hold me there. Water would flow by almost to my waist, but I loved that I would be immersed in the river. For me it was the best seat in the house.

The pre-trip preparation was an army drill in whitewater safety. There were twenty paying customers, with little or no moving water experience, and it was the guide's job to deliver them to Dalton Post safely. Every year people die in the exact circumstances we were about to enter. The difference on the Blanchard/Tatshenshini was that the customers were being guided by men who could interpret the power of water. They had spent years translating the river's secret language and it was up to them to tame her for a paying audience.

Andy and I dressed in the neoprene wetsuits, which were a second skin moving contrary to our own. We went to the water, tried to get comfortable on the cat pontoons, and using our paddles pushed off. Adam maneuvered us into mid-stream, slowly joining the convoy of rafts making its way languorously downstream. It was a thrill to be moving, pulled by a silent current. It was pure motion, movement that could only be verified by the passing landscape.

A kilometer farther on around a sweeping corner, we came upon the first set of rapids. We heard them from two hundred meters away, a hushed roar that grew until we could see them, seething just above the river's horizon, like a gnashing set of incisors.

It was then I realized just how precarious my seat was. Only a single set of muscles was securing me to the slippery hull. I felt like a climber trapped by an insurmountable section of rock, waiting for my legs to break into convulsive contractions. The water's freezing chill disappeared and a flush moved under my wetsuit, adrenaline pumped through my veins, my heart rate soared. I was scared.

Beside me Andy was transfixed, a grin on his face. Above us, on the rowing frame, Adam was a study in concentration. His gaze focused on the water's churning mass, trying to create a map out of the maze of waves, pools and eddies. Using the long steering oars he lined the cat straight downstream. We were headed directly into the roughest section. I was mesmerized. The raft moved in slow motion, its speed seeming not to increase in time with the rushing water around it.

Then Adam leapt up from the frame and shouted, "Hard right, hard right!" We thrashed at the water, the cat shifted perceptibly, but the paddles were getting no purchase in the foamy white water.

Before us loomed a rock, a boulder that had been hidden from farther back by the standing wave. We were making straight for it. I shifted backwards, tensing my muscles, bracing for the impact. The boulder smashed head on into the frame, immediately halting us and hurling Andy head first into the rapids. Adam leapt onto the empty pontoon, his hands outstretched, but Andy was already being pulled away.

We gave the raft a mighty heave and dislodged it from the boulder. Adam shouted at the drifting Andy to keep his feet up. To get caught in the river rocks, pinned under by the rolling hydraulics, was the quickest way to drown. The cat drifted in frustrating, slow-motion pirouettes, but was gradually gaining ground.

Suddenly the seething water around us had no context. The noise and confusion that had absorbed me just a minute earlier was now focused on the body drifting before us. The banks to either side dissolved in a soft focus, the river's angry waves lost their roar. Andy, not the negotiation of the rapids, was now the goal.

On the frame Adam was functioning on instinct, eyes to the river, hands intuitively working the steering oars. In the water Andy was calm. His lifejacket and wetsuit kept him afloat, but the rocks lying just below the surface were battering his body. His face was calm, but each jolt from below forced him to grimace. We maneuvered behind him, like some massive, uneasy space station, and he frantically grasped onto the grab lines of the left pontoon.

He was gasping, but at the same time laughing. "Whoa!" He let out a huge war cry and yelled, "Man, that was a ride."

Andy muscled himself back on board as the catamaran moved on. A sense of relief came over us. The situation had never felt out of control, but there had been a background fear. The power of the river, and the constant subconscious knowledge that we are not creatures of the water, had lent an edge to the experience.

Adam apologized for his navigational mistake, explaining that not having been in white water for three months he was rusty. Paddling combines a knowledge of the forces that a river creates and the ability to manipulate those forces. It is a skill that must be continually upgraded and kept in tune.

As the day progressed Adam regained his confidence. The water became increasingly more difficult, but his improved piloting made the ride thereafter almost uneventful. Adam had been given a swift reeducation, while Andy and myself had been initiated into the cult of white water.

The trip down to Dalton Post took almost four hours and by the time the groups arrived they were soaked and tired. We quickly loaded the rafts onto the roof of an old school bus and drove back to our vehicles at the rafting camp.

The return ride was a chance for the clients to recount the day's events. It was strange to hear people whose entire whitewater experience amounted to a single day labor on about its transportative powers. This,

I felt, was not a good thing. The customers were weekend warriors from a Whitehorse government office, and the guides were not gurus, but young men after a summer paycheck. The guides had learnt to read the river and they had gained a healthy respect for her power, but in the process their skills were used to soften her impact.

Had the impression been given that the river was anything more than a high-priced playground? The thrill of the trip was in the guides' ability to control the water for the client's benefit. But the river was not presented as a holistic entity; it was a ribbon of amusement, a watery roller coaster that was there for the customer's enjoyment, not as an integral part of the landscape that it had helped create.

Neophytes like myself had been given an experience of power in relation to the river far beyond our abilities. It was a dangerous misconception.

Two mornings later we returned to Dalton Post prepared for the twelve day journey down to the Gulf of Alaska. We had made a trip back to Whitehorse for supplies, a crew raft, and the two remaining members of our group, Paul and Coral.

From the roof of the van we levered down the raft, a surprisingly heavy, partly inflated bed of rubber. We dragged it to the water's edge. It was a squat turtle of a craft; the catamaran had been a racing yacht in comparison. It lay flat to the water, no graceful lines to it, pure function, a platform on which to traverse wild rivers. It was gray, a fitting color, being the signature shade of minesweepers and tugs.

Altogether it was six meters long. In its midsection was strapped the rowing frame, the bridge of our ship, the stage from which Adam would direct his minions. On the pontoons, to the fore and aft, squeezed between the various watertight boxes and bags, were our seats. This was the galley's hold and we were now the ship's engines, paddlers to implement Adam's orders in maneuvering the vulcanized beast from shore to shore.

We unloaded a mountain of brightly colored, waterproof bags from the van, but our initial attempts at loading the raft proved futile. There was a system to effective packing, a strategic placement of heavy and much used objects. Adam took command. By 10:30 a.m. we were packed, and with great hoots and hollers and slaps on the back we were off.

The raft rode differently than the cat; it was a transport truck of the liquid highway. The water tugged at its wide hull and our paddle strokes did little to shift its direction.

As a crew we were tight with the tension of learning a new skill. Only Adam was comfortable, leaping around the rowing frame like a wide-eyed child, excited to be back on the water. The rest of us sat squirming in our seats, searching with our rears between stiff pontoons and jagged aluminum boxes for a position that would be comfortable enough for twelve days.

The river was wide and fast but not hectic. We floated easily past a throng of anglers casting spinners and flies out in our direction. Dalton Post is the only accessible Pacific salmon fishery in the Yukon and draws fisherfolk from across the territory. The fishers waved, but it was a half-hearted farewell for they were too absorbed in their pursuit of the river's inhabitants.

Along the banks, forests of white spruce interspersed with aspen and cottonwoods receded up the valley. The trees were undersized old growth, the survivors of cold, altitude and wild fire. It was a forest of dwarfs compared to its southern counterparts. But there was beauty in its asymmetry and a quiet depth in the myths it represented. These were the woods that had provided the Tutchone natives with food, medicine, and protection. The forest was the center of the Tutchone cosmos, a multifaceted emanation of the great spirit.

The forest itself is centered on the river. The moderate microclimate that the Tatshenshini fosters creates the boreal environment. Symbiotically the river also depends on the forest. Fallen logs create oxygen-rich riffles that vitalize the stream; massively rooted cottonwoods gently twist the water's flow and provide cooling shade for its cold-blooded population; and the decomposing leaves of alders and poplars add to the organic matter that drops far downstream, fertilizing berry flats and alder islands. The river and the forest have an understanding, an unspoken synergy that benefits all the species that are attracted to the Tat's gentle climate.

Above us the spruce trees had become watchtowers. On the branches of many were perched stoic eagles, sentinels staring intently into the murky pools, concentrated on catching a flash of rust or pink. The river was alive with spawning salmon. Sockeyes and springs were working their way back upstream, fighting the relentless flow to return to the gravel bed of their birth. In the silted translucence of the river they were streaks of rose electric, dashing from the gentle eddies into their next battle with the current.

But the current was the least of their concerns; it was a constant force beyond any control. On their miraculous migration fish nets, barbed flies, bears, blocked channels, hungry seals, and silted-over spawning grounds were variables of greater weight, all conspiring to cut short the salmon's last and greatest deed.

The fact that so many do reach their spawning grounds is a tribute to the power of personal history, because the route that the salmon re-trace is a memorized map of waterborne scents. In navigating their ancestral passage the fish use olfactory prompts to decipher the river-scape's arteries, veins and capillaries. The odor of the riverbed's subtle chemical changes, particularly at its convergences, are the road signs that direct them to the gravel of their home.

Salmon can swim up to eighty kilometers a day, but it is a death march. To complete the task the salmon, unable to consume enough calories to stay ahead of their bodies' demands, are forced to eat their own flesh. Like the marathon runner, whose only goal is the finish line and who collapses upon crossing it, the salmon will pass on at its own end-point, the site of its once and future birth.

Ahead of us a range of low ancient hills funneled inwards and we found ourselves back within a canyon. Mottled, reddish walls and geometric sandstone hoodoos lined the river, dwarf alders poked up from between the rocks and as the space tightened the river began to throw itself against its steepening banks. Within these confines the flow had increased. Impatient with the geological roadblocks placed in its way the river grew wilder. Boulders that had fallen from the surrounding cliffs, submerged ledges and sandstone outcrops all combined to throw the river into a snarling fit.

It is the river's need to find the path of least resistance, but its physical properties force it to move from side to side. The narrower the space the more dramatic its oscillation until eventually the flow becomes a dynamic, fluid snake rolling against ever-changing borders.

The boat leapt and dropped through the rock garden. Its eddies and holes, an amorphous mass to the crew, were the language of the river for Adam. The throw of a certain wave or a twist of the hull would bring him to bark orders. "HARD RIGHT!" We would lean into the aluminum paddles, watching the shafts bend under the pressure of muscle and water, and slowly feel the raft drift lazily across the biting current.

The bow and stern were interchangeable and the boat pirouetted like a dancing hippo. One second I would be staring into a gnashing hole, the next I would see the view back upstream, and then again I would have to grip the frame as we sideswiped a stone fang protruding from the cliff wall.

I was discovering, by observing Adam, that the maneuvering of the raft had much more to do with his expert manipulation of the long-shafted steering oars than with the crew's thrashing at the waves. The technical sections of white water had to be realized well before we were caught in their midst. The skill was in reading the river, interpreting a set of experientially determined clues and locating us in relation to those. The raft had to be positioned correctly, and held there long before the sucking hydraulics could have a chance to catch a pontoon and throw us to the river's mercy. We were merely a set of thrusters on a booster rocket — Adam was in control.

Forty-five minutes of rough water ended as the canyon cliffs dropped away, and opened out onto the more gentle, montane valley of the Upper Tatshenshini.

We had lunch on the river atop a set of flattened boulders around which the water flowed in swirling eddies. Each of us had our own picnic table, surrounded by an individual moat. We had now negotiated the most demanding sections of white water. Periodic rapids would still appear but nothing as sustained as on the Blanchard-Tat or through the canyon.

After lunch, a lazy drift took us to our camp at Silver Creek. There we initiated the setup procedure that would be repeated each day thereafter. We would drag our equipment and raft far enough up the beach to ensure that a sudden rise in the water wouldn't catch us off guard (the river has been known to flood up to a meter in twenty-four hours). After storing the gear we would erect our respective tents, then search for firewood and fresh water. Afterwards we could relax around a driftwood fire while one of us prepared dinner. And, when supper was complete, there was still lots of time to explore, as the high latitude sun had no intention of disappearing until after 11 p.m.

At Silver Creek we found the remains of an old, long overgrown mining road, undoubtedly the work of prospectors riding memories of the Klondike Goldrush. In 1927 a Tutchone named Paddy Duncan claimed a minor strike just across the river at Squaw Creek. The old trail probably postdated him, possibly the work of the optimists who named the creek by our campsite. Those men were dreamers, motivated by the Klondike legends to withstand infinite hardship, if only for a mere taste of the myths that had inundated their youth.

The next morning we had a leisurely start. The reloading of the raft became a jigsaw puzzle that we daily solved with the dismantling of the camp. One of the beauties of a wilderness trip is that your entire material worth is easily accounted for. Each piece of equipment has a place and there is a place for each piece. The inventory is small and each article has a stated purpose. The simple lack of surplus is something that draws people to the pursuit. The idea that everything of need is within easy reach has a humble attraction. It is manageable minimalism, a simple contrast to the cluttered, possession-driven lifestyles of contemporary culture.

The river after camp was swift but smooth, only slightly marred by the white burst of waves. Once again the hillsides around us contracted as we entered Quiet Canyon. It was a gorge completely different than the one of the day before. The surface was a racing mirror, silver in the new sunlight, but washed by the river's own tensions. The canyon walls were less tangled and the riverside hoodoo spires had given way to gnarled spruce. The trees were eagles' aeries and we were once again the subjects of the great birds' unwavering stares.

Eagles were the cliff's most conspicuous adornment. They peered down at us from their perches, confident that we were of no concern to them. The raft was a passing novelty in their domain, a transient blip in their world of movement. We were neither danger nor food, merely an intrusion that would pass. We dipped our paddles noiselessly, the eagles' haughty stares encouraging us to move on.

Bald eagles are usually a coastal species but they track the salmon upriver, thus becoming a reflection of the fishes' own migration. The Tatshenshini for them represents an everflowing banquet. Its inhabitants are the river's gift to them. Spawning season is their time of feast. They chose their positions on the shady side of the cliffs to get the clearest sightings of the salmon's subtle flashes and those sparks of life become the shivering targets for the hawks' hungry dives.

The bald eagle is the only "fish eagle" indigenous to North America, a species that has adapted to the pursuit of its favorite food. Razor-sharp eyesight interprets underwater movement and curved talons enable them to grip their slippery prey.

Their cousins, the golden eagles, are the true residents of these inland mountains. Their preferred nourishment are the small mammals that inhabit the local terrain: marmots, squirrels and even mountain goats, which they try to force off the cliffs by recklessly dive bombing them from above.

The river opens out after Quiet Canyon, and close to Detour Creek we came across a hunter's cabin. It was a ramshackle array of uncovered plywood and scattered pink insulation. Its foundation lay askew and the structure tilted dizzily to one side. The accessories of the hunt lay tossed around its periphery, empty shotgun shells, moldy outdoorsman magazines, rusty tin cans, and a rotting pair of leather boots. The shack was boarded up, awaiting its owner's seasonal return. After the unadulterated beauty of the river the hovel was a shock, a human blemish that put nature back into perspective.

A few kilometers farther on we came across what must have been the hunter's lookout, a crowsnest of two by four lumber nailed high up in a leaning spruce fifty meters back from the river. We climbed its unsteady ladder and found a fantastic view over a beaver swamp to the north. It was prime moose country, undoubtedly the reason for the lookout's construction.

Moose prefer the thinner snow levels of the interior climate and the abundant aqueous plantlife of the lowland marshes. It is the largest mammal in North America, and the species that resides in the Tat valley is the largest in the world. I have always been attracted to those huge ungulates. Maybe their extreme ugliness endears them to me, or possibly, years before, having been charged by a moose cow for getting too close to her calves, I have a loving respect for their motherly responsibility.

The river, after the lookout, became a meandering, multichanneled flow, interspersed with alder-choked islands. To our east the slab stone flanks of Carmine Mountain came into view, a striking ochre face transected by strokes of green, the traces of the trees climbing its western slopes.

I was caught staring at the massif when Coral shouted to look off to the left. There, in a side channel, was a grizzly, swiping at the water in the throes of the most belligerent fishing technique. Its actions were carefree; it was peak feeding season and with so many salmon in the water it would be difficult for the bear not to eat its fill. But then it caught our scent, and its carefree air was shattered. The bear rose up onto its hind legs, front paws cocked into its chest and threw its massive head back, tossing it from side to side in an attempt to catch a better scent. The ease had left its demeanor and it dropped onto all fours, but then again returned to standing, trying to zero in on the incongruous odor.

This was the "Griz," the species that, because of its incompatibility with humans and need for huge tracts of land, has come to define the North American wilderness. The international reserve strung between Glacier Bay and Wrangell Park is, with its berry-rich hillsides and fish-bearing streams, the perfect home for *Ursus Arctos Horribilis.*

Salmon are an important supplement to the grizzly's diet, but it is almost 90 percent vegetable matter. In the spring hedysarum roots, and in the summer soapberries are its primary foods. To get its fill, a full-grown bear can consume over 200,000 berries in a single day. The Tat and the "griz" are almost synonymous, and the region probably harbors the highest concentrations of these bears in the world.

The bear's second sniff confirmed its worst suspicions and with the verification of the scent he leapt for the shore in a flurry of water and paws. But the current close to the bank was deep and swift and to scramble up the low, reed-covered incline he had to use all his might. We saw his glossy, thickly muscled body flex in graceful ripples, his appendages becoming a definition of strength. Once he'd reached dry land he stopped and glanced back one last time, his coat plastered to him in dark streaks, the water dripping in a profusion of tiny cascades. His fur caught the light and glistened, the muscles of his powerful neck and back were rigid and alert, a thinly rainbowed halo surrounded him from the backlit sun. This was the mythical bear, the native cosmos' statuesque representation of power.

After the excitement of being in contact with such a primordial relative, I felt drained, and was happy that the river would pull us along of its own accord. We wound leisurely through zigzagging streams, the powerful current of the river's upper reaches now lost within the infinite meanders of the widened flood plain. In the distance we got our first glimpses of the St. Elias Range's jagged peaks. To our left the red face of Carmine Mountain grew steadily broader, a massive, slow motion backdrop that defined the scale of the nature we were immersed in.

With so many streams entering the Tat from the west we were worried that we might miss Sediments Creek, our camp for the night. But when we arrived there was no doubt where we were. Sediments Creek is a torrent of thick milk chocolate, its current so choked with silt from the crumbling hills at its source that even though the flow is only ten or twelve centimeters deep it is impossible to see the riverbed. The wide, flat alluvial fan that accommodates its mouth was a perfect campsite and we pulled in for the night.

Soon we would be entering the Lower Tat's moister coastal climate with its almost impenetrable coastal subalpine undergrowth. Sediments Creek was therefore the best place to try and traverse the major ecological zones up through their altitudinal limits and be rewarded with a superb view of the valley. So the next day we planned a hike up to the hills west of our camp.

I woke late the following morning to find the sun was already high and the day heating up. My tent caught the rays, evaporating the droplets of condensation that had gathered during the night. My cocoon was a steaming, green nylon house, its walls shimmering like ruffled silk.

After a breakfast of muffins and eggs we put together a pack for our lunches and followed the creek up into the alpine. A plethora of old bear tracks paralleled the little river into the glaciated mass to the west.

The trail started along the creek's gravel fan. It was a delta in miniature, the result of millennia of erosion eating away at the brownstone canyon that stretched ahead of us. The delta floor was carpeted with bright pink, river beauty blooms that swayed back and forth in a downstream breeze, their graceful wavering a delicate contrast to the unctuous chocolate rush of the creek they bordered.

The track cut into a balsam poplar forest established on a table six feet above the flood plain. The summer woods were a kaleidoscope of color: the purples and pinks of the fireweed and sweet vetch offset the yellows of the arnica and mountain avens, and a multitude of greens in the abundant grasses played against the powdery white of the poplars' trunks.

Farther up the trees ended abruptly and gave way to a grassy open slope. It climbed steeply, but my dreams of a simple stroll to the alpine were dashed when we reached the next ridge. There we clambered out of the balsam zone and into groves of Sitka alder mixed with painfully barbed devil's club. The combination of the two can quickly alter the mood of any hike. The meshed alder branches stymie even the most determined of walkers, while the devil's club needles work their way into the tenderest parts of a person's anatomy.

But the devil's club's diabolic outward appearence is tempered when you discover the native world's belief in its magical properties. It is a member of the ginseng family and up and down the west coast it was used as a cough syrup, laxative, and as a treatment for rheumatism. It is the floral equivalent of the tough doctor.

The subalpine growth thinned out and at around 1,700 meters we moved into the domain of shrubs and dwarf plants. This was the home of juniper, heather, ground berries, and smooth-leafed mountain avens. Even in the seemingly infertile boulder fields we found the delicate white flowers of avens, perfectly centered between their glossy emerald leaves.

The seasonal vigor of the alpine flowers was contrasted with the stunted white spruce. Only in the small chasms perpendicular to the slope, the crevasses that sheltered them from the extremes of the climate, could they survive. They were high altitude bonsais, delicately disjointed masterpieces, surviving on the tiniest window of a growing season.

I climbed a stone finger that jutted from the boulder field — the view in either direction was breathtaking. To the north the Tat wound its way through a wide valley bordered to the east by the Squaw Range and on the west by the Alsek peaks. The valley was lined with easily pitched slopes, mountains that looked ancient and worn. The river in that direction had the lazy look of a prairie stream, weaving back and forth in a gently concave basin, all the while creating gravelly braids that connected the landscape around it.

In the other direction, to the south, the river pushed through an ever tightening valley whose walls increased in scale and steepness the farther you followed its course. These were the main St. Elias Mountains, a younger more aggressive range, jagged lines of crumbling spires with glaciers tucked into the cols between peaks. It was an ominous, geometric landscape. Towards the sea the river becomes a carver more than a wanderer. It grabs the most direct line, pushing its course, forcing the path. To the south the river is an infinite flow of abrading sand and stone, a ceaseless ribbon of the grittiest cut.

In both directions the river is the focus of the land. It is the convergence of terrain, the entity that all else moves towards and the body that directs the topography of its immediate world. The Tat is constantly changing the face of the land it moves through. It is a fluid manipulator in a fluid landscape.

At the base of the stoney knob was a tangled rock garden of shattered stone. The silty boulders were heavily stratified and their exposed layers had been eaten by the wind and rain into a delicate, paper-thin baker's confection. They sat piled against each other like crumbled candy, sweets for the gods. Adam, though, had a different opinion. Thoughts of winter morning newspaper routes crossed his mind: "Hey, looks like the celestial paperboy decided to dump his day's deliveries!"

We lay around the craggy field until the sun was high overhead then started down, dropping back through nature's altitude bands in reverse. On the way back I was shocked by the number of plants and flowers that seemed to have escaped my eye on the way up.

Soapberries, *Shepardis Canadensis*, the grizzly's favorite food, were everywhere, tight red bunches, glossy globules each with a tiny star reflected in its surface. There were white berries too with a pale, snowy texture, cool in the heat of the day, but looking inedible, a potion for shamans. Fungi and lichens exploded up through the mossy undergrowth and clung to rocks and trees. Most conspicuous were the compact clumps of puff balls, perfectly round and slightly stippled, and white toadstools with a burnished sheen and broad concave caps. Each of the fungi was delicately bordered by the mosses and brush that had gently been eased aside during their midnight growth.

Back at the river we had a quick lunch, packed the raft and pushed back into the flow. Just downstream, at Low Fog Creek, we stopped to pick up fresh water. The rivulet flows from the Squaw Range and winds around Carmine Mountain before joining the Tat. It is snow fed rather than glacial, and the lack of silt makes the water almost invisible. Overhanging branches stroked the silent water, contributing just a whispered hint of sound. In the dynamic landscape of the Tat it is a motionless anomaly.

I stood in the creek waiting for the container to fill and the liquid, like glassy oil, wrapped itself around my legs in an icy hug. The water was so cold that in thirty seconds I'd lost contact with my feet. As soon as the bottles were full I raced to the raft, feeling the blood rush back into my appendages like a thousand warm knives.

Ninety minutes farther on and the current picked up. Standing waves could be seen ahead and Adam stood on the rowing frame, straining to get a better look. Like a battleship crew returning to combat we were self-wise and anxious to rejoin the fray. We hit the rapids well. The call from the bridge was "HARD BACK!" and, with our blood running thick with adrenaline, we put our weight into mustering the disobedient craft. The boat was pummeled like a punching bag, but it lazily shifted to the correct line and Adam directed us clear of the heavy water.

About the same time the sun was lost to clouds and the wind picked up. Jeff, one of the daytrip guides on the Blanchard, had warned us that below the O'Connor River the wind could take on hurricane proportions and the entire valley could be gripped by sandstorms. Soon the wind was blowing so hard that it negated the pull of the current. The raft was making no headway. We were halted in midstream. Everything around us was moving, but we were stalled as nature's forces played upon us.

The St. Elias Range is the windiest area in North America. Storms that originate in the Gulf of Alaska blow their way shoreward and get channeled inland up the only available passageway, the Tatshenshini-Alsek valley. These currents, due to the Bernouli effect, gain speed in the confined space and are complicated by the natural downflow of cold glacial currents. The river becomes an arbitrary latticework of blasting winds, dust devils and tiny tornadoes, all randomly rolling back and forth.

Farther down the river, on the wide gravel bars of the O'Connor's outlet, we could see sand squalls developing. The gusts kicked up dirt and silt and whipped them helter skelter up valley. It was an incredible dance of visible energy, a million balls of kinetic potential directed by frenetic forces.

The chaotic wall of gray moved upriver, and we waited for the sandstorm to hit, shrouding ourselves like Bedouin tribesmen. The particles blasted by, filling every uncovered thing with their gritty residue. The river was obliterated, and the water itself took on the matte shade of the atmosphere around it. Air and water came together, losing their individuality, and for a second sky and earth became one.

After the deafening white noise of the storm, the calm after its passing was hyper-quiet. Everything was amplified — the overwhelming visuality of the Tatshenshini for a moment was overshadowed by its soundscape. The brush of water on the raft, the swish of trees on the shoreline, the click of the steering oars against the frame, and the breath moving in and out of my own body were all as tangible as the sight of the river and mountains.

The delta of the O'Connor spread out before us. We looked for a campsite but couldn't find a space that would offer protection if the winds picked up again. Eventually, on the O'Connor's far south shore we found a spot, sheltered by low trees and with a clear creek running close by. Chilled by the wind and soaked by the rapids we built a driftwood fire, and over steaming coffee watched swirling vaporous clouds track the winds upriver.

After dinner I walked up, through willow thickets and subsidiary outlets, to the O'Connor's main flow. Two magpies trailed me, shrieking back and forth, obviously conversing about me, their distinctive cackling and swooping dives a comedy in flight.

The delta stretched for a kilometer along the Tat and in the silty residue of the many dried up flood ponds I found a treasury of animal tracks. Bears were the most conspicuous; dinner plate sized grizzly prints with ten-centimeter claws were mixed with the elongated foot pad of the black bears. There were the big dog marks of *Canus Lupus*, the timber wolf, and the delicate webbed paws of the river otter, whose asymmetrical gait gives its track the look of a dance step. There was the shuffle of porcupines, the light dent of deer and the deep print of full-grown moose making their way back to the marshes. Delicate avian imprints danced on the surface of the mammal tracks, sandpipers, kingfishers, and the more hostile looking claw marks of raven and eagle. The intermingling of them all was a chronological palimpsest of the Tatshenshini's fauna. It was a composition of animals and movement, the imprint of migration and a homage to biodiversity.

From the open ground I could see south and west down the big valley. The O'Connor drainage is the transformation point between the Tatshenshini Basin and Alsek Range ecoregions. Here the shrubby spruce, willow and birch woods of the interior give way to the heavier spruce forests and thick undergrowth of the coastal climate. Downriver the landscape becomes a deeper shade of green as the mixed deciduous forest submits to the coniferous. The mountains themselves become more pronounced. Their younger age makes the peaks appear steeper and more treacherous. The new topography combined with the dense growth at the lower altitudes transforms the Alsek and St. Elias Ranges into impenetrable fortresses.

I returned to camp near sunset. Everyone had gone to bed, but there were embers in the fire, so I put water on for a cup of tea. By the river's edge I sat and watched as a cloud on the far shore wrapped itself around the midsection of a mountain like a vaporous monk's tonsure, a misty crown for a saintly peak. The cloud was soft and light, caught at a consistent level, trapped in a parallel band just at the level of the mountain's alpine line. Below it lay the immersed emerald of spruce trees and above it poked the peak's bald summit. It was contemplative geography caught in its most pensive mood.

The scene struck me. I felt the landscape was seeping into me. The environment was making me more contemplative. The mountain was a reflection of myself, my own mind was being wrapped in thought, watery contemplation on the world that flowed at my feet.

On the river the next day I noticed that the rolling standing waves we had encountered the day before were becoming more frequent. Adam mentioned how the huge volume that the river had now taken on washes out the choppy white water that was common in the upper sections. On the river's lower reaches bed anomalies work on an exponentially increased scale, creating larger and larger rollers with correspondingly powerful hydraulics.

The increased power of the flow also meant that it had more carrying capacity. I had noticed the day before, in the lulls between conversation and storms, a subtle, crackling sound, like electrical static, emanating from beneath the boat. The river was so full of silty debris, suspended because of the dynamic power of the current, that it was grating away at the hull. It sounded like skis on old corn snow, or the snap, crackle, pop of a cosmic breakfast cereal. I enjoyed the sound — it was a techno-beat dialogue between me and the river, audible evidence of its unceasing motion.

We had a short day on the water. There was no goal in mind, and when, close to Tomahous River, a beautiful campsite appeared, we steered shoreward for a look. We pulled in and found, on an elevated alluvial fan, a small abnormally straight creek of pellucid water, each bank lined with groves of river beauties. The decision was unanimous and we unloaded the gear.

It was an interesting spot, as it lay directly across the river from Tats Creek, Tats being the water system down which Geddes Resources Ltd. had been planning to transport ore from a proposed copper mine at Windy Craggy Mountain. The project could have been one of the largest copper producers in the world. Thirty kilometers up the creek an open pit mine would have decapitated the 1,900 meter Windy Craggy Mountain. In the process it would have employed 650 people for twenty years, and produced 20,000 tonnes of ore per day. The total cost of the project was estimated between $400-500 million. It was a miner's dream come true, and yet it never got beyond the planning stages.

The Windy Craggy blueprint was, from an environmental perspective, flawed from the start. The primary stumbling block lay with the fact that the ore was contained in rock that was 40 percent sulfide. That meant that when exposed to oxygen it would produce sulfuric acid. The acid would leach heavy metals out through the bedrock and eventually into the Tatshenshini and Alsek Rivers. This cocktail of acid and heavy metals is lethal to fish, and consequently to every other interconnected member of the Tatshenshini food chain.

To alleviate the problem Geddes recommended eliminating contact with oxygen by building a five square kilometer reservoir and keeping the 375 million tonnes of waste under four meters of water. The pond would be contained behind two earthen dams, one 110 and another 46 meters across but, because Windy Craggy is in the most active earth-

quake zone in North America, those barriers would be extremely suscep-
tible to rupture.

The second major concern was with the transport of the ore. To
get the concentrate from the mine site to the U.S. port at Haines, Alaska, the company would have to build a hundred kilometer road and a
405 kilometer mile pipeline for dewatering the slurry. Both would have
had immense impact on the wildlife in what is now North America's
largest protected wilderness.

Moreover, a 210 meter bridge across the Tatshenshini above the
O'Connor and a twenty kilometer access road along the river would
have destroyed the "wilderness experience" that adventure outfitters
were selling their clients. The mine would have had a fifteen to twenty
year lifespan, after which the landscape would have been altered forever.
In contrast, provided it can utilize an intact environment, the wilderness
"industry" can operate indefinitely.

It was a question of short term investment and return as opposed
to a sustained long term commitment. The Tat is now a biospheric museum, one of the few spaces left on earth in which to observe an environment unscarred by the heavy hand of man.

The opposition to the mine site was international and focused.
On June 22, 1993, it was announced that the entire watershed would be
protected within a 9,580 square kilometer park. In 1994 it was designated a UNESCO World Heritage Site. The announcements were a tribute to the activists' belief in the importance of the river system and to
the Tatshenshini's own beatific magnetism.

At the campsite I pitched my tent close to the banks of
the little creek. Inside I was serenaded by the sound of fast water mingled with the murmuring rumble of its particulate load. I spent the late
afternoon inside reading, the doorway forming a half-moon frame onto
the dancing waters and their kaleidoscopic banks.

At one point the picture took to motion as a trio of hermit thrush-
es hopped into sight. Picking flies and ants off the sun-hot rocks, their

tremulous, graceful movements a Chaplinesque pantomime. Ignoring me they went about their business, focusing on the life directly in front of them, unaware of the pleasure they created with their presence.

After filling myself with bookish thoughts I took a walk and became intrigued with the size and formation of the alluvial fan that we were camped on. The creek, which was tiny in comparison to the Tat, had somehow created a scarred triangle of stony ground, which, where it touched the main river, was over a hundred meters wide.

The delta was made up of a huge selection of stones, from fine silt and sands to boulders a meter in diameter. Somehow, with the floods that occasionally ripped down its course, the Lilliputian stream had torn the sides out of the mountains above us and dragged the results kilometers down to its outlet. Looking at the size of the scars on the mountainsides and comparing it with the scale of the creek I was shocked. The water's manipulative potential seemed completely out of sync with the sylvan stream that lay before me.

The little creek described for me, in a manageable form, water power. The Tat and its capabilities were too huge to comprehend, but that seasonally ravenous little spring had shown that it could pull the guts out of the land around us. The creek made me look at the Tatshenshini with heightened appreciation.

But the most beautiful part of the creek's geological legacy was the depositing of the debris from its fluid rampages. When I stepped down off the alluvial plateau I could see, in the two meter high swath that the Tatshenshini had cut across the rocky fan, centuries of stone deposits striated one layer on top of the other. Each pebble appeared to have a predetermined place in the crosscut, each stone was encased in an exposed shell of hardened silt, and each individual rock sat perfectly placed in relation to the hundreds of thousands of others trapped in the stony timeline. Like the layers in the glacier's depth the stone mural was a visible description of the creek's life, a fresco of the stream's accomplishments.

After dinner I went to meditate and found a perfect place to sit on the edge between the forest and the stony delta. There, in the transition between the two, I identified a fear that had been stalking me for days. It was not a specific concern about bears or the danger of the water itself, but the fact that we were so far removed from the modern facilities that "tame" the wilderness. Naiveté or faith had brought us four days from the nearest civilization without a can of bear mace, a VHF radio, or even an axe. We had no way to call for help if a problem occurred, we had no way, beyond our bare hands, to fend off a bear attack, and we were alone and adrift on humankind's non-element. The wild loomed untamed and raw before me. In my meditation I saw it as our ancestors would have, a towering presence, unavoidable and overbearing. We were there only with nature's grace and would continue on down the river only with her consent.

Fear — it was something that our ancestors always felt consciously or unconsciously towards the earth. Nowadays we feel as if we've conquered nature. I thought of a recent *National Geographic* advertisement, "In the 20th century man conquered nature. In the 21st century, we'll help protect it." In the stillness by the creek, looking out over the devastation wrought by a babbling brook and with my body bristling in anticipation of the first sounds of bear or cougar, the conquering of the world around me was as distant as the boardrooms of Washington, D.C.

Late that night, around 1:30 a.m., the call of a different nature dragged me outside. The sand was cold under my bare feet, and I was enjoying the release of a tight bladder when I looked up, and for the first time in those high, summertime latitudes saw the moon and stars.

The moonlight reflected on the river's shadowy flow, the water caught the pale luminescence and threw diamond shot spray at the night. The crystal sparks danced against the far, darkened shoreline, while overhead the stars winked, silently appreciative of the river's choreography. I traced the depthless sky down to the unending ridgeline silhouettes, the blackness lightening with the descent, until at the horizon, hovering between earth and sky, lay a thin line of palest blue. That was the far north, the Arctic, the land of the midnight sun.

I was sad to see the little stream and its perfect alluvial fan drift behind us, but the ocean was pulling and it felt right to move on. We had another late start, but that was no problem — there was no schedule and daylight was as long as we wanted it to be. The river was the underpinning of the time we were working in, a constant reminder that everything moves on. The river was our clock and we moved within its framework.

The Tatshenshini was widening; tributaries like the O'Connor, and the Tkope were adding their volume and creating a vast river. We were now into the main St. Elias Range, and all the peaks around us were adorned with glaciers, hanging ice fields poised between summits like divine jewelry. So much ice, and so much water. Those mountains were beautiful but possessive. They grasped their fluid component, unwilling, except for a few months in the year, to permit the thaw and let their waters rejoin the perpetual flow to the sea.

It was to be a short day: we only needed to reach the confluence of the Tatshenshini and the Alsek. We arrived at the junction without fanfare, but I was shocked by the immensity of the meeting place. The Alsek arrives majestically from the northwest. It is a river with purpose, a flow without the Tat's rushed edge, but a river whose majestic scale mimics its origins in the vast Yukon interior.

With the confluence the river more than doubles in size. Looking down the valley it was hard to fathom the amount of water that was being channeled through those mountains. Before us was a moving sea, enough water to satisfy a small nation, and yet for days there had been not a single human permanent resident to appreciate this desert dweller's dreamland.

The river had become a world unto itself. In the flow with us were all kinds of floating debris, logs and branches, leaves and dry grass. I had to wonder if, to the river, our raft was just another piece of refuse, flotsam being moved by its unending power.

There were rumors of a petroglyph on an island at the meeting. This was intriguing as it would be the first human evidence since Dalton

Post. At the confluence there were in fact two small granite islands. We stopped at the first but could find no sign of a rock carving, and so with Adam steering and his crew working double time, we maneuvered across the convoluted currents to the second islet. At first glance there again we had no sign of petroglyphs but on its northern shore there was a fantastic campsite, so we beached the raft and hauled our supplies up the beach.

Afterwards I joined Adam and Coral on a more intensive search for archeological remains. I struggled to the far side of the island through thick coastal underbrush, devil's club and alder mixed with head-high fireweed and ferns. My bushwhacking led out onto an open slope of magenta river beauties, an angled pool of color leading down to the water.

The meadow was inundated with bear sign: trodden brush and fresh tracks criss-crossed the opening. There was a tension in the air; whether it was self-created or from being watched, I couldn't tell. I hurried back to the camp site, anxious for company.

I returned to find that, on a clean rise above the tents, Adam had uncovered the petroglyph. It was on the highest point of the granite knob, a faint, chiseled dot encircled by two rings, from which emanated a set of muted rays. It was a sun, undoubtedly a symbol of power in a land that, for much of the year, is shadowed in cloud.

It was such a simple design and yet almost impossible not to be moved by it. It was the first sign of anything more than a transient human presence that we had seen in five days. The artist would have been using stone tools to carve in stone, and imagining the amount of time involved and the commitment to the goal was awe-inspiring.

The question of why raised itself. Was it penance, an offering, or pure obsequience that had motivated the person? At first it appeared out of place, timeless handiwork in a land beyond humankind's presence. But it was not always so. The carving was evidence of the culture that had once thrived along the banks of the Tatshenshini and Alsek. The positioning of the petroglyph, on an island between the two fluid axes of that world, added even more complexity to the enigma.

There is evidence that the valleys were inhabited as early as eight thousand years ago and the separately distinct cultures of the coastal and interior peoples were established around 2,500 years ago. By the mid-nineteenth century the Tat-Alsek area, because of its salmon rich streams and berry thick hillsides, is thought to have harbored the highest concentration of aboriginal peoples in British Columbia north of the fifty-ninth parallel.

The corridor became a major trade route between the Tlingit and the Tutchone. Every winter the coastal Tlingit would walk up the frozen river as far or farther than Neskatahin, near what is now Dalton Post. There they would stay until trading was finished in late spring or early summer, and then canoe back downriver to Dry Bay on the Pacific. The Tlingit would also visit interior villages during the summer fishing season, as it was much easier to dry their fish inland for the long winter.

But by the end of the nineteenth century the entire valley south of the Klukshu River was completely deserted. The abandonment was not the result of a planned exodus or some far-flung government relocation plan but the culmination of two catastrophic events — one that, in a single sweep, wiped out life on the Alsek, and another that, over a period of years, insidiously destroyed the fabric upon which millennia of culture had been built.

The first was a massive river wave that occurred between 1848 and 1891. It was then that the Lowell Glacier, known as "Naludi" or "fish stop" in Tutchone, surged across the Alsek and dammed the river. Behind it built up a huge reservoir of glacial water which inevitably ate into the ice dam and caused it to give way. From behind the wall a towering wave of water, hundreds of meters high, crashed down the valley, destroying everything in its path. The results can be seen to this day on the walls around the confluence. There you can see an eerily distinct difference in the size of trees above a parallel band a hundred meters up from the river. This was the height of the tidal wave whose deadly wash swept the valley clean.

On the granite island itself the scour marks of debris that crashed along with the flood are still noticable on the knob's surface — a tracing of cuts torn into solid rock, evidence, 150 years later, of the power of the event.

No doubt, the "Gunana" Tutchone village that is thought to have existed at the meeting of the rivers was obliterated in an instant. All that remains of that world is one faded reminder chiselled in stone.

The second great catastrophe to strike native culture on the Tatshenshini was the meeting of whites and the natives. The aboriginal environment was devoid of most of the socially communicable diseases that afflicted Europeans. The two cultures' interaction brought syphilis, measles, mumps, diptheria, scarlet fever, influenza and, most fatally, smallpox into the native world.

In 1861 a Russian Navy estimate set the aboriginal popluation at 7,389; by the U.S. census of 1891 it had dropped to 4,583. George Thorton Emmons was a United States Navy lieutenant stationed on the northwest coast at the turn of the century. He mentions seeing "whole villages depopulated, the timbers of the buildings rotting, the longhouses empty shells." In their weakened state there was little the once proud Tlingit culture could do to resist the onslaught of white society.

That night was a magical descent to darkness. We were caught in the audible jaws of two great rivers, surrounded by the sound of unstoppable flows. Overhead, streaky clouds shot with the extended colors of the northern twilight mirrored the flow of the earthly currents. They clashed, mixing and transforming, becoming what we wanted them to be, vaporous avatars of celestial rivers. Sky and earth moved together, touching at the distant ends of the rivers' worlds.

The following day we floated lackadaisically down to the Walker Glacier area. Around noon we caught up to a party of rafters from Alaska and Montana. They were older folks whose time on the river was a cherished respite, a time to quietly contact the parts of life they were forced to subvert in their everyday existence. These were a different type of tourist than the daytrippers on the Upper Tat. For the daily whitewater runners the river was a playground, for the longer expedi-

202

tioners the river was a refuge. Now that the river is a protected area it has become a destination, a place to plan an excursion into the wilderness. The Tatshenshini-Alsek is a drawing card, a Mecca for outdoor enthusiasts in search of wilderness solace.

We drew up alongside the lead boat and the guide apologized for "swarming" us with their four rafts. We laughed, happy to be in contact with a group that shared our feelings for the river. They were enjoyable people with a great combined knowledge of the region; there were biologists, hydrologists, a meteorologist, and experienced kayakers. We chatted amongst ourselves as the river kept pulling us on.

The Americans eventually drifted to the right bank as we hugged the left. Strange, as we were about to cross the border between Canada and the U.S. somewhere around us on the forested hillsides was a line cut by a survey crew decades before to signify the point of transition. We squinted and stared but could discern no evidence of the crossing between nations. We entered America silently, without visas; there was no one present to complain.

Once into the States the river made a sharp swing to the southeast and when we had completed the turn we found ourselves staring at Walker Glacier.

Even from water level it was impressive. The ice towers, or seracs that denote where the frozen river tumbles over the lip of its moraine slope, stood out like a fantastic set of shattered teeth. The glacier itself was cupped between two impressive mountains, each with their own respective sub-glaciers. The icefall blocked any views of the Walker's origins. Its source was a mystery, a shadowy space that would require further effort to decipher.

We pulled into the campsite beach and set up our tents. From my nylon house pitched tight into the hollow on the lee of a sandy hillock, I looked directly south at the glacier's ragged face. Closer in, a foot from my doorway, two bees were tucked snugly into the underside of some scarlet red Indian paintbrush. The flowers swayed ecstatically in the breeze, the bees riding out the cold winds gusting down from the icefall. Off to my left a pair of magpies argued, dogfighting above a tiny pond, screaming with a vicious avian edge. Between the tent and its fly sheet grasshoppers leapt, bouncing back and forth between the layers of fabric, making it pop sporadically like a loosely strung drum. The little hollow was alive with its own personal ecosystem.

The boulder-scattered moraine fields leading from the glacier to the river were a lunar landscape alive with color and light. The rock darkened ice of the glacier's lip transformed into a network of lakes and ponds. The stoney tarns melted into boulder fields, which in turn disappeared into an undulating set of sand dunes, and it was the dunes that became the banks of the Alsek.

Scattered between this geological microcosm were tracts of wildflowers. Daisies and monkshood swayed beside fireweed and river beauties, their movement a trembling juxtaposition to the solidity of the stone they rose from. Around them clumps of alder and thickets of aspen were dispersed, the trees adding height and depth to the Walker's ever changing moods.

That night I fell asleep with my tent door open. Two hundred meters south the lake at the glacier's base ate away at its frozen banks. Mammoth chunks of ice rolled in slow motion tumbles into the water. Their entry was heralded with the sound, a million times amplified, of ice cubes swishing in a glass.

At the same time on the darkening massif to the Walker's south two peaks cradled a hanging glacier, and as I looked on a bomb of stone and ice plummeted from its face. The displacement rumbled around the valley like echoing thunder. These were the loudest sounds I had been subjected to in the past week. It was as if, after millennia encased in ice, the water was noisily objecting to its reinstatement into the cycle of elemental stages.

The next morning, starting at 10 a.m., we threaded our way through the maze of eskers and dunes and traversed the ice lake up onto the glacier's tongue. It was a rolling, frozen field that ended abruptly in the icefall. The ice was smooth and firm, like the surface on Datsalaska Glacier, but, where at the source there had been but a single mushroomed rock for us to lunch on, here there where dozens. Interspersed between the rust and gray toadstools were moss and lichens, displaced blasts of green prospering in an almost soil-less environment.

Around these alien fixtures flashed fissures coursing with water, aquamarine clefts colliding together in smooth unison. The sound of water was mixed with the cool wind dragged off the upper ice. Gothic spires, tunnels of ice, otherworldy mushrooms — the tongue was a Zen garden of vaguely familiar images.

At the icefall we found that the seracs were hundreds of metres high. From the river they'd appeared as scaleable boulders of ice. The seracs we now saw were Gothic spires, frozen cathedrals teetering on the edge of equilibrium. In their bodies was a compressed display of the glacier's history exposed through time to the forces of change.

To circumnavigate the ice towers we climbed a waterfall on their right. The seracs became more impressive the closer we approached, for their scale, even up close, was difficult to comprehend. They absorbed the world around them. It was a landscape so confident in its possibilities that size was a secondary concern.

Glacial action is one of the most potent geomorphological forces in the Tatshenshini-Alsek watershed. The last great de-glaciation was approximately 12,000 years ago. That event, the shift in climate and its consequences, is the basis for the topography that is seen today. The residual glaciers, the last vestiges of that time, continue to exert incredible influence on the local environment.

The region has one of the highest concentrations of surge glaciers in the world, possibly thirty-one of the 350 ice floes in the basin are of this type. A surge field, unlike a normal glacier, can move relatively quickly, in surges, and, like the Lowell field on the Alsek, can cause major damming on the river itself. The catastrophic effects of the release of those reservoirs, like that at the confluence of the Tat and Alsek, can be seen throughout the area.

Once above the icefall we scrambled along the moraine to the glacier's left. That upper moraine was the granite effluent of the Walker's advance. The rock was dredged from the depths beneath the ice and in its journey to the surface crushed to pebbles and dust. It was there that you could conceive of the glacier's power. At the moraine edge you could see its ability to grind and alter the land it rolled over, to take boulders the size of houses and turn them into silt.

Along the glacier's shifting borders, scrambling through loose scree, we continued on to another waterfall that crept down to the ice floor from the hills to its north. Here Adam and Andy decided to traverse the ice floe. They set off on a path of their own design, tracing the high ground between the crevasses, leaping clefts and sidestepping chasms. They became lost to us, absorbed in the jumble of ice and rock that congested the Walker's surface. Finally we glimpsed them again on the far shore, now looking like ants on the horizon. We had been fooled again by the ice floe's scale. Against the backdrop of the hanging glacier above them and the river of cracked ice before us they were specks of dust, blown there by a glacial wind.

From the moraine Paul, Coral and I decided to move up the side hill in search of a panoramic view. Picking our way through mossy granite and unfettered stones we followed the little waterfall to where it connected with an esker paralleling the path of yet another glacier-fed stream. Here we stopped to admire what was laid out before us.

Below us the Alsek pushed on to the southwest past subsequent ice floes and wooded flats, massive and yet dwarfed by the peaks around it. To the southeast the Walker Glacier continued back and around a ragged ridge that hid its ultimate source.

From above, the jungle of distressed ice and rock was transformed into a graceful floe contained between twin lines of noble peaks. You could see, in the perpendicular fissures created by the crevasses, the movement of the ice. You could recognize how this was, in fact, a frozen river, a watercourse that desired to move but was inflicted with a river's greatest woe, a temperature below zero.

After lunch, taken in a meadow of scarlet fireweed that angled down to the glacier at thirty degrees, we made our way back to the moraine and tracked it towards the icefall. In the process we met with the group of the Americans from the day before. They were in a heated discussion with a lone German over the future of the electric battery.

The German man had invented an ultra lightweight, aluminum cell and had brought it to the Alsek to test it in the "Vilderness." The battery for the Amercians was a piece of the consumer dominated world they were trying to get a temporary release from. It was a talisman of our uncontrollable need to tame the wild, to control the wilderness and dilute its potency.

The conversation brought to me memories of John Muir and a conversation he had had a century before with a Tlingit shaman. The shaman had said, "It has always seemed to me while trying to speak to traders and those seeking gold mines, like it was speaking to a person across a broad stream that was running fast over stones and making so loud a noise that scarce a single word could be heard." The shaman had seen the white traders and gold rushers as too busy to engage in a dialogue with nature.

We separated from the group as the conversation was getting heated, and moved down over the icefall to the tongue. Compared to the topographic confusion of the upper floe the lower section appeared smooth and ordered. In the afternoon heat the ice had taken on a glassy sheen. I stopped frequently, attracted by the debris that was trapped in the translucent mass: ghostly lichens, shards of moss, globs of soil, twigs, and fragments of wood. Most intricately preserved, however, were leaves that had blown up from the riverside groves, aspen and alder folioles that had been scoured by wind and time into fossilized remnants. They were skeletal relics of the trees' tremulous solar panels encased in ice. There was no way to know how old those floral bones were, from the year before or ten thousand years ago. It was no matter, for they were poetic archeology, and the dates could be left to the scientists.

Past the tongue we retraversed the stone mushroom gardens, circumnavigated the ice-lake that ate its borders, and were finally back onto terra firma. With soil underfoot a sense of constancy returned, but at the same time the idea that something the size of the glacier was in constant motion challenged thoughts of nature's immobility. Everything, the glacier had proven, is in a state of flux, from the river, to the ice, to the rocks that pulsated around us. The land was alive with potential energy.

At camp after supper we were treated to a display of vaporous art that proved the point. Drawn by the jet stream coursing off the Gulf of Alaska, then beaten against the peaks of the St. Elias, the wispy clouds that had followed us all day were forged into the shape of otherworldly UFOs. With the consistent cooling of the evening air the ethereal formations stabilized over the river and were injected with the golden light of evening. In the tradition of the Aurora Borealis it was an archetypal northern light show, a rainbow shadow dance reflecting the mutability and depthless scale of the world it hovered over.

We awoke the next morning to find that the cloud play of the night before had been the harbinger of a change in the weather. The sun had disappeared, and in its place was a deep fog that hung to the river and eliminated depth perception. It had rained in the night and at breakfast our crew resembled a gang of stumbling zombies. We shoved off into a thick pea soup, not quite knowing what the day would bring. Such a simple change in the climate had altered all our moods. Being at the whim of nature brings a person into contact with one's own barometric temperament.

On the water all was silence. The river had lost its voice in the mists and with it so had we. We stared into the fog trying to pull features from the limitless gray. But there was nothing; the trees and rocks on either shore had been absorbed into the clouds that had come to earth.

Even the river, the flow that had been our constant companion, was difficult to discern, for its gray was diffused with the same shade of sky. It was an invisible automaton pulling us on. The questions of how or where, the queries that had for the past week been on all our tongues, now left us.

The fog lay in low striations, rising and falling with imperceptible currents. A layer would hold, like solid steam, over the water, then a strata of clear air might expose a band of trees, but, above that, low cloud would blanket the hills on either side. There was water everywhere, river, streams, trickles, mist, fog, cloud, ice, snow, and the dense moist air that we were breathing. But now that air was tinged with the smell of salt: somewhere close by was the great repository, the mother ocean.

At one point we caught sight of an eagle, stoic and intent on a sandbar, while overhead a seagull dive-bombed it. The gull's courage was commendable, its attacks relentless, but soon we realized the reason for its persistence: the eagle was feasting on the gull's chicks. In the gray light the dark side of nature was exposed.

By mid-afternoon we had reached the spit of land around which the river flows into Alsek Lake and there we decided to stop for the night. The lake is the centerpiece of a dramatic basin whose entire western rim is a border of ice. This is where the Alsek Glacier unloads into the frigid waters. We set our camp at the far southern edge of the sandy peninsula, making sure to pitch our tents at least six feet above the waterline. Gerry, the guide for the American rafts, had told us of two meter rogue waves ploughing across the Alsek Lake in the aftermath of a serac tumbling from the ice floes.

Again my tent had an incomparable view. Even in the dim light I could make out, to the south, the surreal shape of Gateway Knob, the 155 meter knoll that marks the exit point of the river and the apex of the Barbazon Range that leads to the northwest. Panning west from the knob across the lake I saw icebergs stilled in the dull waters, unmoving like huge multi-masted ships becalmed in a fog. Farther west the lake dissolved into grayness, its far shore lost in the haze. To the north the edge was visible and banked with forest. The shores there were littered with beached icebergs, scuttled like a fleet of phantom battleships.

My lullaby that night was the sound of the calving glaciers, great seracs toppling to the water with the crack of a Howitzer, and with each repeat I wondered if this would be the one that spins the rascal wave in our direction. Between the shots and the reverberations that rattled the valley I could hear the static fizzle of precipitation on my tent. The rain had come. The weather gods were welcoming us to the coast.

The next morning we packed the raft and paddled in the direction of the glacier. The river current was lost in the lake's volume, so for the first time in weeks we would be self-propelled. Within half an hour my arms were aching and I was wishing for the river's return.

We rowed out of the silt brown flow of the Alsek and into the bluish milk tinge of the lake itself. Halfway to the western shore we spotted a Gothically shaped iceberg, a massive rugged triangle with a symmetrically rounded orifice carved through its main body. It was a cathedral of ice moving, in complete silence, across a matte mirror of still water.

Our initial thoughts were to scale it and claim a waterborne summit. But as we moved closer, silently approaching an object that demanded quietude, we could see that it was all a dream. The iceberg, like the ice fields to its rear, defied all perspective. The berg that we thought was the size of a large boulder was, in fact, closer to the size of a four-story office block. Our ideas moved to the ridiculous and we began to laugh, realizing we were the victims of a wish that nature had no intentions of fulfilling.

We paddled close into the "holey" berg. In its wind shadow the water was dead calm, but off gargoyle cornices and through the gap notched in the massif the breeze sang unearthly songs. It was a beautiful siren calling to wayward crews. We circled it, but it was too large a piece of ice to fathom. We took it in piece by piece, a subtle notch of aquamarine here, a gravel-scattered plane there, a rounded stone boulder defying gravity by hanging from shards of ice.

We pulled away, as we had arrived, slowly and in silence. But that day the iceberg never left us. It was the focus of the lake, at times shrouded in uneven mist, at others radiating with a hidden light, and at one point the blessed recipient of a single, mist-defined shaft of sunlight.

We rowed for the far shore, for the glaciers that had birthed the iceberg. The raft moved sluggishly through the gray-green water, the liquid seeming thick and viscous. The bow wave was a muted roll, our craft ploughed instead of cut through the water, and behind us a trail of slow bubbles marked our passage. Our arms were telling us that we were moving at a fair clip, but the glaciers were not getting any closer. Once again their scale dumbfounded us. Why was this ice so difficult to fathom, why was its size so far beyond our comprehension?

Eventually we arrived, but the constant explosions of the calving process made us wary and we stayed fifty meters back from the face. The wall fluctuated between fifty and 150 meters high and its frontispiece was a work of art. On the Walker the icefall had been ripped and torn into a convoluted mass, but here the Alsek's ice face had been cleanly cut. You could view the entire chronology of the ice floe from the water. Through the face rode lines and shades, colors meshing from above and below. It was all angles and soft curves, dropping to a point where liquid lapped at solid. The glacier was the simultaneous repository of frozen time and time in transition.

We pulled away around a headland, and as the glacier passed from view the drizzle turned to rain. The mist had turned to solid and we were caressed by the softest waters. It was a gentle fall, a butterfly's kiss in comparison to the falling waters of the glacier. The tiny liquid eggs wrapped around my face like cold puppy licks and entered the green waters as perfect divers, no splash, no noise.

We recrossed the river and landed on Gateway Knob. Camp was set against a thick scrawl of alder that pushed up a steep hill. The north slope was a tangle of coastal underbrush, but to the south, trapped in mist, wind-beaten spruce hung tight to the ragged bluff. It was a scene from a Schzewan painting, brush strokes and water in shades of gray.

The rain sang at dinner and followed us to our tents. Around midnight the dream of a waterworld became a reality as I woke to find my tent inundated by puddles and pools of cold water. Dozily I woke, went outside, and moved my nylon house out of the depression. I lay back down again shivering, only hoping for sleep to take the chill away. The river was steeped in my dreams.

At 10:30 a.m. we stole away from Gateway Knob under our own power. Behind us the icebergs still stood as misty guardians, and the glaciers continued on with their business of the explosive rebirth of ancient waters.

The larger bergs were too deep to make it into the river. At the lake's outlet they gathered, and sometimes created a jumbled mass that dammed the flow and raised the lake level dramatically. The thought was shocking because the river at that point was over two hundred meters wide, and a phenomenal amount of ice would be needed to chock its flow.

After fifteen minutes we were back into the river's current, and could again stow our paddles, put our feet up and let the Alsek pull us into its dewy netherworld. Ahead was the sound of fast water. To either side we were being passed by room size chunks of ice, submerged crystals, windows onto the muddy flow. Rapids loomed, and the boat waded through them with a joyful batter of bodies. To our left, at one point, heaving masses of ice were trapped between rocks, and white water flooded over and around them, an infinity of liquid hands dragging them back to their origins.

Downriver I could hear big rapids. I stood and reached over to tie in my cameras and when I brought my head back up was dumbfounded to find the raft perched on the lip of a three meter standing wave. The obscenity that left my lips was lost to the river, and, with the world around us a boiling caudron of water, I saw Adam, working the oars and laughing like a madman. He was loving it.

The wave marked a transition. Soon after, on the left bank, a large log cabin appeared. It was the first glimpse of permanent habitation in almost two weeks, a seasonal hunting lodge with gargantuan moose antlers hanging over the door. On the lawn, by the river, a small gunpowder cannon sat while on a flag pole close by the Stars and Stripes and a black and white Jolly Roger flew together. Our first sight of stationary life was of a Yankee pirate.

We began to see incongruous shapes looming out of the fog, square shacks, triangular lean-tos and crosshatched fish drying racks. The geometric imperialism of western civilization had made its imprint on the Alsek delta. In the water we saw nets and buoys, fluorescent intruders in the milk chocolate flow. Strangest of all, however, was the distant sound of outboard motors. From deep amidst the fog, riding above the acoustic rush of the river, was the staccato whine of internal combustion engines. The song of the river was being heckled by the sound of a million mechanical mosquitos.

Along the shore the mountains had given way to low hills and soon they too disappeared into the extreme flat of the delta. As we floated by, the geographical work of the waters became evident. Entire banks dropped away into the flow. Trees, their roots eaten away by it, stood at ragged angles, and clumps of grasses and shrubs lay half submerged in the river.

Here too were strong signs of the power of the earthquake, the water's geomorphological complement. The St. Elias Range is one of the most active earthquake zones in North America. To the west lies the Hubbard/Boarder fault and to the north and east the Denali fault. Moreover, 150 kilometers to the west lies the Yakutat Gap, one of the most powerful geologic forces in the world.

The riverbank in the delta makes incongruous leaps in height. From close to river level the shore jumps five or six meters for no apparent reason. These fluctuations are the signs of a huge quake in the late 1950s that completely altered the immediate landscape.

It was then that the East Alsek, originally an outlet course of the main river, was separated from the larger flow. A tectonic rise placed an insurmountable obstacle between the two rivers, an almost incomprehensible feat considering the scale of the Alsek at that point. The separation has distanced the two watercourses, not only geographically, but also geologically. The main Alsek is a thick, silt-laden rush that chews away at the land around it, while the East Alsek is a clear, rain-fed stream only twenty kilometers long, a river with even, gravelly beds that, in its short course, supports over five times the main Alsek's population of salmon. For the seasonal fisherman of the area the East Alsek is a river of gold, while the main Alsek is a river of danger.

Through the fog we were able to find our way into the main flow's elusive left channel. This was the sluice that would lead us to our final take out. If we had missed it the river would have pulled us all the way out to the ocean, and from there it could have taken us days to drag our boat back up to the airstrip where our ride back to Whitehorse would be landing.

Ahead we could hear the diesel roar of a seasonal fish processing plant close to the airstrip. Adam directed us into an eddy and suddenly we were unloading the raft for the last time.

With the fogs still unfurling all around but our tents pitched and talk of supper plans still hours away, Adam and I decided that we should complete our trip and walk the last six kilometers out to the ocean.

We crossed the airstrip and followed a path lined high with alder and young spruce. The entire flats had at one point been logged and the homogenous stand of fifteen meter evergreens were evidence of the regeneration. Soon, though, they gave way to stunted coniferous shrubbery, gnarled and buffeted by the salt-laden sea winds. Sheltered amongst these, however, fireweed and small blooms of heather still glowed. But eventually even these petered out and we found ourselves crossing a windswept desert of sand squalls and low gravelly knolls.

Around us fog raced, while pieces of driftwood and dried plants rolled by. On the open flats, unencumbered by trees, the winds could play unobstructed, and it was there that I could feel the sea in my bones. Now there was a rich salty taste in the air and a palpable warm mist clung to my exposed skin.

From the desert we crossed some low dunes sprouting with rugged elephant grass. Ahead of us were the skeletons of ancient fishermen's shacks. The wooden frames hung dark against the lightened mist. They were weather-beaten and coarse, angular protrusions from a flowing landscape. They had held no inhabitants for years and inside one a wood fired "Arctic Stove" lay open and full of blown sand.

Here we came across the tracks of some mammoth grizzlies, their huge paws almost the size of Adam's feet. The tracks took off across the wastelands in the direction of the ocean and the sight made me think of how a bear must view the land. Does it discern beauty, or does it define the landscape constantly in terms of food and danger? We were wary now; the dunes were not a place to confront a bear. We were completely exposed, and in that landscape a meeting of us and them would have left the humans as the inferior cousin.

Over the last set of dunes we came to the sea. The sound we had heard at our camp six kilometers away finally had a source, and it was deafening. The sight of the sea itself was shocking — it was a snarling mass of foam and water. It was ferocious and chaotic.

The waves hit the beach in continuously random leaps, and the force that they brought to bear on the stretch of sand was altering the land before our eyes. They rolled in like foamy tongues, lapping at the pulverized earth and pulling it back down into the depths.

There, with the sea erupting out of nowhere, its cacophonic chorus driving away unabated, the sky seemingly emanating from the gray waters, and the beach a child of the frenzied tides, it was simple to see the sea as the primordial mother, the universal one from which all began.

Epilogue

My long sleek sea kayak glinted in the autumn sun, the sea was just barely chopped, gentle rolling waves moved me and a light breeze pulled the tops of the whitecaps up to lick my face. My paddle strokes were the focus of my being. I would drop the blade down into the viscous green water, let the river get a cold grip on my hand and then, evenly and cleanly, I'd pull the shaft back along the hull. I moved at a comfortable pace dictated by the dialogue between my body and the water.

The sky was clear, a transluscent aquamarine reflection of the river. On the shore the city had encroached on the water — apartment blocks and parks, docks and marinas, factories and log booms dominated the foreshore. On riverside paths people walked, while in the background cars moved quietly by. Out in the bay I could see a scattered collection of freighters, a ragged gang of unmoving steel behemoths waiting silently for their loads. Beyond them the mountains of Vancouver's North Shore formed a verdant, mysterious backdrop in the low-angled sunshine.

One hundred meters away I spotted what had brought me out on to the water that day. Ahead was the barely moving, half-submerged body of a man. He was swimming slowly his arms plying into and out of the water with simple precision. Each stretched, windmilling stroke pulled him closer to his goal. He wore a bright green wetsuit, the black hood of which covered his head and gave him a surreal, alien look. His face was obscured by a diving mask but as I drew closer I could glimpse his eyes through the glass. I could see he was in his own world, his focus was on something distant, something I could not see. Ten meters away a half-dozen people on his whitewater support raft shouted encouragement, playfully cajoling him on, but he was oblivious — his only mission was to keep pulling himself forward. The man was caught in the interzone between land and water, his only focus was movement. I stopped paddling and let the waves rock my boat. I was mildly shocked, the man seemed so removed from my landlocked reality. The shore was only one hundred meters away but here was someone who was transcending the boundaries between fish and mammal.

The man in the water was Fin Donnelly, a former competitive swimmer who has become one of Canada's more effective river activists. Fin's best publicity weapon is his swimming ability. On the day that I met him he was just completing a four-week 1,400 kilometer swim from the headwaters of the Fraser River to its outlet at the Pacific. The route would take him from the rugged peaks of the Rockies and the boiling whitewater of Hells Gate Canyon, to the fertile farm lands of the lower Fraser Valley and eventually to the river's mouth on the south side of the city of Vancouver. In the process Fin would get to see the river in all its forms. Over almost a month of swimming he would get to know its moods and feelings, its dark sides and its compassionate self. As he told me, "When I do these swims I obviously develop an intimate connection to the river. I learn quickly to work with the river's dynamics, to become part of the river."

Swimming the length of one of North America's great rivers is not the kind of task most people would think of undertaking, but Fin is unique — some call him a revolutionary. He swims such incredible distances to raise public awareness of the problems of the river and the communities on its banks. Fin swims to remind us of how we affect the rivers we live along. He is the medium through which the water can be heard.

I asked Fin if he had seen any changes in humankind's relationship with the Fraser during his ten years as a watershed activist. "The Fraser River is still a sewage pit," he told me, "but I think we are slowly awakening to the fact that we are exerting a tremendous impact on rivers. . . . We realize things must change, the question is can we muster the will and change quick enough."

The statement hung with me, for it was a point that I had been wrestling with since I began my river journeys two years before. Could we reverse the destructive attitude that had brought about so much suffering to the watersheds I had seen around the world. I thought about the altered landscape of the Rhine, the years of effort that had been given over to changing its flow. I was brought back to the Tatshenshini and the ongoing fight to keep it pure and unadulterated, and my thoughts lingered on the Ganga and of how contemporary Indian society has relegated the fluvial mother goddess to background iconography.

It was painful to dwell on those thoughts but Fin brought words of hope, "I believe there is a growing awareness of the damage we are causing and an increase in the realization that we need more respect and care for the environment. However, there is an equally strong contingent focused on driving consumption through the roof. . . . It will be interesting to see which path humanity chooses."

I thought back to that first vision of the Ganges from the plane high above its delta, of how I had seen the streams and channels as mirrors of my own circulatory system, and of how I had felt a direct connection between the river and my own body. Then I glimpsed what Fin had experienced on his months in the water and of the motivation that now drove him to protect the riversheds of his home — I saw that if we couldn't change our attitude to the river, we would in the end be killing a part of ourselves.